Berlin

Jack Altman

CITYSCAPE

JPMGUIDES

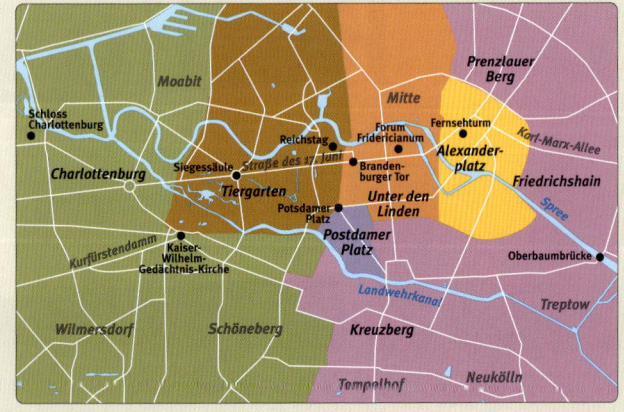

Germany's capital is huge. You can get around quickly by underground or overhead trains, or by hopping onto a bus or tram. To save you some legwork we have grouped the sights by district, starting at the centre with the Brandenburg Gate.

Contents

Features

Music in Berlin	36
An ever-changing skyline	44
Remembering the Wall	54
Berlin for children	66
Retail therapy	78
Kartoffelpuffer	108
Berlin on the screen	117

Maps

1 Friedrichshain, Kreuzberg	129
2 Mitte	130
3 Charlottenburg	132
4 Berlin	133

Fold-out Map

City Centre
U-Bahn and S-Bahn

Symbols

- ★ Our favourites
- **U** U-Bahn
- **S** S-Bahn
- **Tram** Tram
- **Bus** Bus

cityLights	5
cityPast	9
citySights	21
Unter den Linden	22
Alexanderplatz	38
Potsdamer Platz	48
Tiergarten	56
Charlottenburg	68
Prenzlauer Berg, Friedrichshain and Kreuzberg	80
Excursions	88
cityBites	99
cityNights	111
cityFacts	121
Index	134

cityLights

This is not a town you can pin down. You can never say at any one time what Berlin is, only what it's *becoming*. Germany's capital offers constantly stimulating reminders of the unstable soil of swamp and sand into which it has sunk its foundations. Berliners are used to seeing their buildings knocked down, by war, by imperial and communist despots or capitalist speculators, then resurrected or replaced by something equally grandiose, outrageous or, at times, just banal. Look away for a moment and everything changes: now it's the capital, now it isn't, now half is the capital of a truncated country, the German Democratic Republic (GDR or East Germany), and half—on the other side of the infamous Wall—is a beleaguered Western frontier town in the Cold War. Today, after seeing off both the Wall and the GDR, Berlin is once more the proud capital of a whole country.

Focus Shifts East

The town is jumping. The construction boom of the 1990s has not let up. The vast Potsdamer Platz, a bleak wasteland throughout the years of the Wall, has returned to being a throbbing centre for entertainment and commerce, with new theatres, hotels, cafés, bars, restaurants and a pleasant shopping mall. To meet the transfer of government and its bureaucracy from Bonn, the venerable Reichstag parliament has been gutted and renovated, new ministries and embassies built, and others reclaimed. Superb art collections, split up during 50 years of the Cold War, have been reunited in new museums, while old ones have been restored after decades of neglect.

Historically, Berlin has always had more than one "centre". In 1920, the creation of Greater Berlin united 8 towns, 29 rural communes and 27 independent districts. Today, of all the many changes, one of the most remarkable has been the revival of eastern Berlin. After years of being dismissed as dreary and characterless, with at most the curiosity value of a Stalinist stronghold, the "east" has seen its neighbourhoods of Mitte, Friedrichshain and Prenzlauer Berg thrive again with boutiques, art galleries and restaurants. It has regained something of the vibrant atmosphere it enjoyed in Berlin's Golden Twenties.

The Kurfürstendamm, Western Berlin's glitzy boulevard, the smart side streets of Charlottenburg and chic Savignyplatz now face competition from the new and refurbished buildings on Unter den Linden, Friedrichstrasse and the less flashy but increasingly lively area around Kollwitzplatz in the east. Even the gigantic apartment buildings on Karl-Marx-Allee that served as a showcase for bombastic Stalinist architecture in the 1950s have had their façades spruced up.

Not all is new. Many of the finer Prussian monuments of the 18th century still stand: the Hohenzollern monarchs' summer residence, Schloss Charlottenburg, the Brandenburg Gate leading to Friedrich the Great's edifices on Unter den Linden, the elegant Gendarmenmarkt's French and German cathedrals flanking the Konzerthaus (the Schauspielhaus at the time). And not all is charming. Hitler's Olympic Stadium has been transformed into an ultramodern venue for the 2006 World Cup, but the Nazis' bleak and soulless office buildings on Leipziger Strasse, Fehrbelliner Platz and Platz der Luftbrücke still stand much as before.

Theatre, Music and Cabaret

Berlin is once more at the centre of the country's cultural scene. Performing in the acoustically magnificent Philharmonie concert hall, the Berlin Philharmonic remains one of the world's greatest orchestras. Germany's leading actors and an enthusiastic public are drawn to plays at the revived Berliner Ensemble created by Bertolt Brecht, the innovative Schaubühne, and the energetic Deutsches Theater founded by Max Reinhardt. And the city's famous summer Love Parade brings ravers from all over Europe and beyond.

Germany is not famous for its sense of humour. Berlin is. This is quite an achievement, considering the stiff and starchy Prussians who historically made up the city's ruling class. The *Berliner Schnauze* (Berlin lip) has always been part of the turbulent city's survival kit. In the 1920s, its citizens' sardonic wit made itself most keenly felt in the satirical cabarets. If Hitler disliked Berlin so much, the people's humour was certainly partly to blame. Taxi drivers, street vendors and bartenders are as mordant as ever. After a long period in the doldrums, the cabarets have bounced back, relishing in particular the arrival of the federal government with its inevitable scandals and power struggles.

Melting pot

With a population of about 3.5 million, Berlin is a sprawling metropolis and, like London, a city of boroughs, many of them veritable villages. The city is delightfully green and airy. Lakes, forests and parks cover over a third of the metropolitan area. Berlin is flat, but the rubble of Allied bombardments in World War II was used to form artificial hills: the Teufelsberg in Grunewald or Mont Klamott in Friedrichshain, providing good viewpoints and acceptable ski slopes in the winter. Southwest of the capital is the old Prussian royal court city of Potsdam, easiest of leisurely day trips.

The end of the Cold War also restored to Berlin its pivotal role in relations between eastern and western Europe. A glance at the telephone book reveals the quantity of Slavonic names. Poles, Russians and citizens of many of the old Soviet republics are a fixture of the Berlin scene. Notably, the arrival of Jews from these countries has increased their community, numbering only a few hundred survivors after World War II, to over 12,000. The largest "foreign" community is Turkish, mostly living in Kreuzberg.

cityPast

Signs of people living in the area date back over 10,000 years, but it was not until well into the Middle Ages—the municipality's modern name was first mentioned in 1244—that anybody could honestly say *"Ich bin ein Berliner"*. For most of its history, the city as we know it now was a cluster of highly independent-minded villages founded to exploit the fishing and trading facilities of the Havel and Spree rivers and surrounding lakes. In fact, some of them, like Charlottenburg, Wilmersdorf, Schöneberg, Köpenick and Spandau did not become part of Berlin until 1920. Those Stone Age nomads left flint weapons and a few reindeer bones, but the first real settlers, around 3000 BC, were probably farmers.

An early Germanic tribe moved into the southwest district of Teltow in the 6th century BC. In the 6th century AD, colonies of Slavonic Sorbs began settling in Köpenick on the Spree River and Spandau on the Havel.

Middle Ages

The thriving Slav communities of farmers and craftsmen—skilled weavers, potters and carpenters—were in turn absorbed by tough migrant German merchants in the 12th century. They came from the Rhineland, Westphalia and Saxony, followed later by others from Thuringia. From the Ascanian dynasty in the Harz Mountains, Albrecht the Bear provided Berlin's future emblem, ruling the surrounding state of Brandenburg as its first margrave (1157–70).

It was only in the 13th century that the city began to take shape in the loose association of its component communities. Cölln was a fishing village (now Fischerinsel) on an island in the Spree. The Mühlendamm embankment linked it to the township of Berlin on the north bank, where travelling salesmen found hospitable inns and rental carts for their merchandise. Its marketplace around the church of St Nicholas has been reconstructed as the quaint Nikolaiviertel tourist area.

Berlin and Cölln joined forces in 1307 to combat bands of highway robbers upsetting their trade with Poland. They built a joint town hall on a bridge between the two townships, with two councils governing in tandem. The system worked well enough for them to join, in 1359, the prosperous Hanseatic League of cities trading from the North Sea and the Baltic.

The Hohenzollerns Move In

In the 15th century, Hohenzollern princes from south Germany took over Brandenburg. They made their home in Berlin-Cölln and cut back the dual township's municipal autonomy.

During the Reformation, the Berliners re-asserted their independent spirit by forcing Prince-Elector Joachim II to embrace the Protestant creed of Martin Luther in 1539. Their motivation was not so much religious as practical, but nonetheless high-minded. The money they saved on Catholic church taxes served to turn a monastery into a printing press and publishing house and to found a secular high school (*Gymnasium*) next door.

The Thirty Years' War (1618–48) gave no reason to be high-minded about religion. The city was laid waste first by the Swedish troops of Gustavus Adolphus, who championed the Protestant cause, and then by the Catholic army of the German Emperor. Plague, famine and war cut the population in half, from 12,000 to 6,000.

Capital of Prussia

The city began to take on the appearance of a real capital under Friedrich-Wilhelm, the Great Elector (1640–88). He added fortifications, planted trees from his castle to the Tiergarten along the avenue that was to become Unter den Linden, and above all took drastic measures to increase the population. In 1671, he welcomed some 50 wealthy Jewish refugee families from Vienna. They were followed by nearly 6,000 Protestant Huguenots driven from France after Louis XIV revoked the Edict of Nantes. Later, other Protestants joined them, coming from Switzerland and the Rhineland Palatinate. These newcomers—many of them sophisticated merchants, jewellers, tailors of high fashion, gourmet chefs—brought a refined, cosmopolitan flavour that was rare in other German cities of the day. By 1700, the population numbered over 50,000.

The Great Elector's son inherited both Brandenburg and the eastern German territories of

Friedrich-Wilhelm (1688–1740)
Friedrich the Great (1712–1786)
Otto von Bismarck (1815–1898)

Prussia in 1688. Since the latter also included Polish lands, in 1701 he crowned himself King Friedrich I *in* but not *of* Prussia. He let his energetic wife Sophie Charlotte guide him in founding Berlin's academies for the arts and sciences and commissioning great baroque architects like Andreas Schlüter. The royal palace, the Berliner Schloss, was destroyed in 1951, but other buildings on Unter den Linden and the queen's summer palace, Charlottenburg, testify to this first flowering of Prussian splendour.

Their frugal son Friedrich-Wilhelm I (r.1713–40) cultivated a new and more rigid spirit of Preussentum *(Prussianness)*. He preferred beer to wine, the barracks to the palace. After his coronation, the Sergeant King, as he was nicknamed, sold off his robes and the royal silver to pay off his extravagant parents' debts, and ordered his courtiers to dress in military uniform. He turned the royal pleasure-garden (still known as the Lustgarten) into a parade ground, and in his mother's gardens at Charlottenburg planted cabbages in place of flowers.

Friedrich II (r.1740–86) duly rebelled against the stuffy philistine legacy of his father's court. He practically abandoned Berlin to devote himself to creating in Potsdam an elegant but more intimate version of Louis XIV's Versailles. The language at his Sanssouci Palace was French, and Voltaire was its honoured resident philosopher. A writer and musician, the king also proved himself a much more brilliant soldier than the Sergeant King—always contemptuous of his son's "effete" manners—ever imagined possible. His victories in Silesia in 1745 earned him the title of Friedrich der Grosse (Frederick the Great), King *of*, and not just *in*, Prussia.

Berlin itself did benefit from Prussia's grandeur as a capital of the Enlightenment, with Friedrich adding to Unter den Linden the grand opera house *(Deutsche Staatsoper)*, buildings that are now part of Humboldt University, and above all the Brandenburg Gate, begun just after his death.

Uniting the German Nation

Napoleon's humiliating victory over the Prussian armies in 1806, underlined by his arrogant entry into Berlin through the Brandenburg Gate, stoked the fires of a new patriotism after the French were driven out of Germany in 1813. Authoritarian Prussia was worried by the nationalist movement's demands for a constitutional monarchy and freedom of the press. These subversive ideas rapidly spread through Berlin's university, founded in 1810, and *Lesecafés* (reading cafés), where intellectuals found in foreign periodicals the news denied them by the capital's strict press censorship.

Unease grew in high places as the new proletariat created by the Industrial Revolution doubled the city's population to more than 400,000 in the first half of the 19th century. In 1848, workers demonstrated at the palace against factory and living conditions. The Prussian cavalry opened fire, killing 230 people. After granting concessions to liberal demands, the government went on to increase press censorship and police repression of political meetings. Workers' housing was barely improved by the grim tenements known as *Mietskasernen* (rent barracks), first appearing in 1862.

That same year, Otto von Bismarck became Prussia's Iron Chancellor and set about appropriating the German nationalist movement for his king Wilhelm I. After decisive Prussian-led victories over Austria and France, Wilhelm was proclaimed Kaiser (Emperor) of the German Reich in 1871, and Berlin became its increasingly prosperous capital. It was the era of department stores and mass-circulation newspapers. Following the route of the new railway linking Berlin to Potsdam, the entrepreneurial bourgeoisie erected its villas around the Wannsee lake and the Grunewald forest southwest of the capital. Bismarck had the Kurfürstendamm built to emulate Paris's Champs-Elysées. But the boom of the Reich's Gründerzeit (Founding Years) also led many to financial ruin and caused mass unemployment.

To counter the rampant materialism of these early years as the political capital, Berlin began to assert its cultural status. The arrival of Viennese director Max Reinhardt at the head of the Deutsches Theater in 1905 inspired it to become the top theatre city in Europe. Tchaikovsky, Richard Strauss and Grieg worked as guest composers for the Berlin Philharmonic. Artists Max Liebermann, Max Slevogt and Lovis Corinth contested Munich's leadership in German painting. In the sciences, winning Nobel prizes was a local sport—Robert Koch was awarded his for discovering the tuberculosis bacillus, Max Planck and Albert Einstein for their work in physics. It was said that of the ten people who understood Einstein's theory of relativity, eight lived in Berlin.

War and the Republic

World War I began in euphoria, with crowds cheering Kaiser Wilhelm II on the balcony of the Berliner Schloss. The grim realities of food rationing and thousands killed on the western front soon turned popular feeling against the war. The Spartacus League of Rosa Luxemburg and Karl Liebknecht, the precursor of the German Communist Party, organized worker opposition which culminated in a strike of 400,000 Berlin workers in January 1918.

By November, returning soldiers had joined workers to fly the red flag of revolution, riding through the streets with machine guns mounted on their trucks. But the political left was split. On November 9, Liebknecht stood on the balcony of the Berliner Schloss, with the crowds this time cheering the proclamation of a Soviet-style socialist republic. That same day, the anti-Bolshevik Social Democrats (SPD) had already gathered at the Reichstag to proclaim a German Republic—and they held the reins of governmental power. Chancellor Friedrich Ebert let his defence minister Gustav Noske call in 4,000 right-wing *Freikorps* militia to crush the Spartacists. The storm troopers assassinated Liebknecht and Luxemburg on January 15, 1919, just four days before parliamentary elections. Reichstag deputies moved temporarily to Weimar to vote the constitution for the new republic.

The "Golden" Twenties

Governing the Weimar Republic in Germany's first shaky experience of parliamentary democracy, Berlin presented a stage that was both frightening and exhilarating. The SPD's use of the Freikorps to defeat their rivals set an example for the right-wing Kapp Putsch of March 1920. The attempt by 5,000 storm-troopers to impose a civil servant, Wolfgang Kapp, as puppet chancellor lasted only five days, but their helmets provided a significantly more enduring emblem: the swastika adopted by Adolf Hitler's Nazis. Political assassination became commonplace. Notably in 1922, foreign minister Walther Rathenau, a cultivated liberal Jewish industrialist, was shot dead in a street near the Grunewald. The struggle to redress defeated Germany's position in the international arena was waged against a background of economic crisis. Bankruptcies and crippling inflation beset Berlin just as it was incorporating into one metropolis scores of suburban villages and hitherto autonomous townships like Spandau, Köpenick and Charlottenburg, doubling the city's population to nearly 4 million.

The turbulence marking the new-found democratic freedoms also proved enormously creative. Wilhelm Furtwängler reigned at the Berlin Philharmonic, and Bruno Walter, Otto Klemperer and Erich Kleiber at the Opera. From 1919 to 1932, the city staged world premieres of 12 major new operas. Culturally, 1920s Berlin was the most exciting city in Europe. And the craziest, too. The paintings of Otto Dix, Max Beckmann and George Grosz, and the brutal photomontages of John Heartfield mirrored the harsh realities of the times. But as a Dadaist forerunner of the Surrealists, Grosz might also be seen staging with writer Walter Mehring a race between a typewriter and a sewing machine. Nightclubs served up whisky and cocaine, striptease and ferocious political satire. In the theatre, Reinhardt's grandiose commercial productions gave way to the revolutionary dramas of Erwin Piscator and Bertolt Brecht, accompanied by the acerbic music of Kurt Weill. Josef von Sternberg's film *The Blue Angel* (1930) symbolized the changing Prussian image with the seduction of the professor (Ernst Jannings) by the cabaret singer (Marlene Dietrich). Berlin cinema was at its height, and Hollywood could scarcely wait to get its hands on directors like Fritz Lang and Ernst Lubitsch.

Hitler made it all possible. In 1926, he sent propagandist Joseph Goebbels to direct operations in Berlin, where Nazis and Communists fought bloody street battles. The Nazis gained the upper hand by exploiting divisions among their opponents, and artists and writers, Jewish and otherwise, fled the capital.

The Third Reich
On January 31, 1933, President Hindenburg's duly democratic appointment of Adolf Hitler as German chancellor was celebrated by a torchlit parade of Nazi storm troopers through the Brandenburg Gate. A fire in the Reichstag

a month later gave Hitler the pretext he needed to impose a tyranny of terror. The Dutch communist arrested on the spot claimed that he was working alone, and a communist plot was never proved; nonetheless the Gestapo secret police proceeded to crush all political opposition. Communists and Social Democrats were sent to the newly opened concentration camps, of which Oranienburg, just outside Berlin, was one of the first.

In May 1933, Nazi students marched along Unter den Linden to their university to burn books of Jewish, humanist and other subversive authors. Jews were systematically excluded from public life. During the triumph of Berlin's 1936 Olympic Games, *"Juden unerwünscht"* ("Jews undesirable") signs vanished from cafés, hotels and shops until foreign visitors left town.

Any international illusions about the fate of the Jews ought to have been dispelled on November 9, 1938, when the Nazis spurred on crowds to burn synagogues and smash and loot Jewish-owned shops all over the country. *Kristallnacht* (Crystal Night), as the event became known, earned its name from the broken glass of a huge chandelier in Berlin's Wertheim department store. Just over three years later, in an elegant Wannsee villa, Adolf Eichmann received instructions at a ministerial conference to organize the "Final Solution of the European Jewish Question". Berlin's Jewish population was reduced by extermination and emigration from 160,564 in 1933 to 7,272 in 1945. (After the creation of the state of Israel, only a few hundred remained, until immigrants from the former Soviet Union brought the number back up in recent times to some 12,000.)

A furious Hitler could not understand why, unlike in 1914, Berliners did not cheer the 1939 mobilization for World War II. In retaliation for the London Blitz, British bombardments in August 1940 quickly brought the war to the home front. By 1945, Anglo-American air raids and Soviet ground shelling had reduced much of the city to rubble. On April 30, as Soviet troops advanced through the streets, Hitler committed suicide in his bunker below Wilhelmstrasse.

Split by the Cold War

Situated entirely within Soviet-occupied East Germany, Berlin came under four-power control after the wartime Allies' Potsdam Conference of 1945. The Soviet-controlled eastern sector covered almost half the city's total area, while American, British and French sectors soon came together as West Berlin. This truncated capitalist metropolis was a constant thorn in the flesh of Moscow's communist regime. The 1948 Soviet blockade of road, rail and waterway links to West Germany was broken by American and British planes airlifting daily supplies of food and industrial equipment. East Berlin was proclaimed capital of the new German Democratic Republic in 1949, with veteran Stalinist Walter Ulbricht as its leader, while West Berlin became a rather garish showcase for Western democracy.

In 1953, an uprising by East German workers against Stalinist repression and wretched living conditions was crushed by Soviet tanks. Protest continued with the flight of nearly 3 million East Germans to the West by 1960. The loss of highly qualified engineers, doctors and skilled workers was costing the GDR millions of marks invested in their training. Soviet leader Nikita Khrushchev instructed Ulbricht to stop the haemorrhage by closing the East-West Berlin border. The massive Wall that grew out of this border closure became a symbol of the Cold War, both of the bankruptcy of the communist system and the Western democracies' cynical acquiescence in the status quo.

Only foreigners and West Germans could cross into East Berlin at special checkpoints. West Berliners had to wait till their former mayor, Chancellor Willy Brandt, broke the Cold War ice in the 1970s. In hindsight, his *Ostpolitik* (Eastern Policy) of forging links with the Soviet bloc was an essential step in bringing down the Wall itself.

Bringing It All Together Again

Erich Honecker succeeded Ulbricht in 1971. He made a vain effort to stay afloat by artificially pumping up a woefully inefficient and corrupt economy, leaving the GDR as grotesquely bloated as its muscle-bound Olympic athletes. The East Berliners' new television sets only served to show they could get much better cars, refrigerators and stereo equipment on the other side of the Wall. From 1987 to summer 1989, a new wave of refugees

made its way to the West via Poland, Czechoslovakia and Hungary. After Soviet leader Mikhail Gorbachev came to Berlin in October 1989 and let it be known that Soviet tanks would no longer protect the GDR, Honecker resigned, soon followed by his government. The Wall fell on November 9 (its site has been marked out in paving stones, as a memorial to this dark chapter of the city's history).

Striking while the iron was hot, Chancellor Helmut Kohl pushed quickly for unification. It was celebrated at the Reichstag on October 3, 1990, and Berlin was again proclaimed the nation's capital. Nine years later, a Social Democratic chancellor, Gerhard Schroeder, ushered in the government move from Bonn to Berlin.

Since 2005, the occupant of its Chancellery in the Tiergarten, aptly symbolizing the new, unified Germany, is for the first time a woman, Angela Merkel, born in Hamburg before moving to Brandenburg in East Germany.

As people concentrated on the building boom, with ministries, embassies, office blocks and new housing shooting up all over the city, a problem still remained of integrating east and west Berliners. The Wall may have gone, but the social, economic and psychological differences of 45 years of separation are still a reality for many. Others see a positive sign in the fact that eastern Berlin's Mitte and Prenzlauer Berg have become fashionable places in which to live and have fun. Now, the east is "in".

Today, the city that seemed condemned to remain a provincial backwater in its Cold War years is again a vibrant, cosmopolitan capital.

◀ *The memorial to the murdered Jews of Europe.*

citySights

Unter den Linden 22
The historic centre east of the Brandenburg Gate

Alexanderplatz 38
A glimpse of life in former East Berlin

Potsdamer Platz 48
Lively, ultra-modern district in the heart of Berlin

Tiergarten 56
From the Kulturforum to the Reichstag

Charlottenburg 68
The modern shopping district

Prenzlauer Berg, Friedrichshain and Kreuzberg 80
Atmospheric neighbourhoods

Excursions 80
Köpenick, Spandau, Dahlem, Grunewald, Wannsee and Potsdam

CITYSIGHTS

UNTER DEN LINDEN

East of the Brandeburg Gate lies Mitte (Middle), Berlin's historic centre. Its prestigious avenue, Unter den Linden, is lined with banks, ministries and luxury hotels. About half-way along, the avenue is bisected by Friedrichstrasse, a vital north-south thoroughfare. To the north, around Oranienburger Strasse, is the old Jewish quarter.

THE DISTRICT AT A GLANCE

SIGHTS

Architecture
Gendarmenmarkt ★ .26
Alte Bibliothek 26
St.-Hedwigs-
Kathedrale 26
Prinzessinnenpalais ...28
Schlossbrücke..........28
Berliner Dom 29

Browsing
Friedrichstrasse........25
Oranienburger
Strasse ★ 32

Entertainment
Tacheles – Internationales Kunsthaus ..33

History
Unter den Linden ★ .25
Staatsoper Unter den Linden 27
Friedrich the Great Monument..............27
Humboldt University...............27
Kommandantenhaus................28
Schlossplatz 29

Memorial
Denkmal für die ermordeten Juden Europas ★ 24
Neue Wache............27

Landmarks
Brandenburg Gate ★ .22

Pariser Platz.............24
Neue Synagoge........33

Museums
Madame Tussauds ...25
Zeughaus, Deutsches Historisches Museum 28
Museumsinsel ★ 29
Altes Museum 31
Alte Nationalgalerie 31
Pergamon Museum 31
Museum Blindenwerkstatt O. Weidt ..32

WALKING TOUR 34

WINING AND DINING 100

Brandenburg Gate (E3) At the entrance to Berlin's royal avenue, Unter den Linden, this grandiose monument, completed in 1791, carries on its broad neo-classical shoulders the full symbolic weight of the city's history. Carl Gotthard Langhans' design was inspired by the gatehouse to the Parthenon in Athens. The Doric columns are flanked by what were originally a Prussian Army guard-

The Brandenburg Gate has become a symbol of two cities united.

house and a tollbooth for collecting customs duties. The bronze Quadriga—representing Winged Victory driving a chariot pulled by four horses—was intended by the sculptor, Johann Gottfried Schadow, to symbolize peace, as depicted by the procession he carved beneath it in sandstone, and if his wish had been granted the gate would have been called Friedenstor (Gate of Peace). But the Prussian kings saw it as a monument to celebrate their wars, for which they commissioned the gate's other friezes. They also replaced the wreath of olive leaves in Victory's hand by the Iron Cross (removed after World War II and restored in 1990). Napoleon led his victorious army through the gate, as did his conqueror at Waterloo, Field Marshall Blücher. Other marches here demonstrated for freedom—against the Prussian monarchy in 1848 and against the Stalinist regime in 1953—but also for tyranny, with the Nazi torchlight parade of 1933. In 1989, the gate proved a natural magnet for crowds celebrating the fall of the Wall between East and West Berlin. It has become a symbol of the nation's unification, and the emblem on Germany's Euro coins.

TRAVELLING QUADRIGA

Unlike most equestrian statues, the bronze Quadriga that Johann Gottfried Schadow created for the Brandenburg Gate really moved around a lot. Coming to Berlin after his victories at Jena and Auerstedt in 1806, Napoleon carried off the Winged Victory and her horse-drawn chariot back to Paris. She might have ended up atop the Arc de Triomphe looking down the Champs-Élysées if the Prussian Army had not conquered Napoleon and marched into Paris in 1814 to carry her back to Berlin. There she and her horses were restored to the Brandenburg Gate. A persistent urban legend of the Cold War had them once more on the move, turned around by the Communists to face defiantly into West Berlin—only to be turned back again at reunification. Not true.

Denkmal für die ermordeten Juden Europas (E4) Inaugurated in 2005, the Memorial to the Murdered Jews of Europe stands near the Brandenburg Gate. It consists of 2,711 grey concrete slabs of varying height. American architect Peter Eisenman has created a grid pattern on gently and unevenly sloping ground that has a slightly destabilizing effect on visitors walking among the stelae. The abstract symbolism of the work is explained in the underground information centre, which also documents the destinies of individuals and whole communities in the death camps. • Stelae accessible round the clock. Information centre: daily except Mon. Apr–Sept 10am–8pm, Oct–Mar 10am–7pm (last entry 45 min before closing) ☎ 26 39 43 36 • Ebertstrasse Ⓢ Unter den Linden 🚌 100, 200, TXL, M41, M48

Pariser Platz (E3) Reduced to rubble in World War II, the square immediately east of the Brandenburg Gate is assuming once more its role of "drawing room" (Salon) for the grand Unter den Linden avenue. Framing the gate, two sandstone mansions have been rebuilt in their patrician 19th-century style: to the left (north), the Max-Liebermann-Haus, where the Impressionist painter lived for 40 years; to the right, its twin, Haus Sommer. On the square's southeast corner, the monumental **Hotel Adlon** has re-opened to welcome well-heeled guests. They have a hard act to follow: the Rockefellers, Lawrence of Arabia, Albert Einstein, Charlie Chaplin and Enrico Caruso. The Akademie der Künste (Fine Arts Academy), the French embassy, bank and office buildings have arisen on their original sites. The new American embassy opposite opened in July 2008 on the site of the original, which functioned from 1919 to 1941; it had to be redesigned for security reasons after September 11, 2001.

Unter den Linden (F3) Now that some of its finest historical buildings have been refurbished, this grand avenue is recapturing some of the grandeur of its Prussian heyday. It began in 1573 as a bridle path for the Hohenzollern princes and courtiers riding to the Tiergarten hunting grounds from the Berliner Schloss. The avenue's name derived from the 1000 lime or linden trees added in 1647 by Friedrich Wilhelm, together with 1000 nut trees. It was the only thoroughfare in Berlin that really interested Friedrich the Great; he laid out his **Forum Fridericianum** halfway down, with buildings that now form part of Humboldt University. At the avenue's western end, near Pariser Platz, is the Russian Embassy, a characteristic Soviet monument completed in 1953, year of Joseph Stalin's death.

Madame Tussauds Berlin (E–F3) This new Tussauds exhibition opened in Berlin in July 2008. Some 80 wax figures, most of them representing German personalities from the realms of history, politics, culture and sport are displayed in interactive tableaux. You also get a chance to look behind the scenes and see a wax figure in the making. • Daily 10am–7pm (last entry 6pm) ☎ 40 00 46 10 or hotline 0180 5 54 58 00 • Unter den Linden 74 Ⓢ Unter den Linden 🚌 100, 147, 200, TXL

Friedrichstrasse (F2–5) Since the city's reunification, Friedrichstrasse has taken on a dazzling new character. It had always been, from the mid-19th century on, the town's busiest shopping, café and theatre street, but also the sleaziest. Today, it has been rebuilt, like Potsdamer Platz, by the world's top architects, with the city's smartest boutiques, shopping arcades, luxury hotels and fine restau-

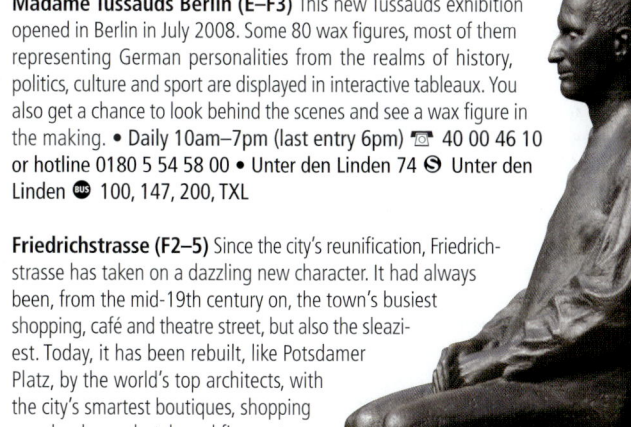

Bertolt Brecht sits outside the Berliner Ensemble.

rants. The Friedrichstrasse area has four prominent theatres. On the north bank of the Spree on Schiffbauerdamm is the Berliner Ensemble, created by Bertolt Brecht, whose square is nearby. A short walk to the northwest, along Albrechtstrasse, is the Deutsches Theater founded by Max Reinhardt, and the Kammerspiele. Back on Friedrichstrasse is the bold and brassy Friedrichstadtpalast variety hall.

Gendarmenmarkt (F4) Turn south down Charlottenstrasse to reach this graceful square. It was laid out in the early 18th century for twin baroque churches commissioned by Friedrich I. On the north side, the Französische Friedrichstadtkirche (1701) was a gift to Huguenot Protestants who had fled Louis XIV's France in 1685, while German Lutheran community of Friedrichstadt were given the Deutsche Kirche (1708). Between 1780 and 1785 the two churches were completed with domed towers, and since then they have both been called a "Dom", which usually means cathedral but in these instances, refers to the architecture. The tower of the **Französischer Dom** now houses a Huguenot Museum, while the **Deutscher Dom** is the setting for an exhibition of the German Parliament, documenting the development of a parliamentary democracy. Between the two buildings stands the splendid neoclassical **Konzerthaus Berlin**, originally the Schauspielhaus, built by Karl Friedrich Schinkel in 1818–21.

Alte Bibliothek (F3) The graceful curved façade of the old royal library, now serving Humboldt University, was inspired by the baroque wing of the Hofburg Palace in Vienna. In the middle of **Bebelplatz**, a monument by Israeli artist Micha Ullman (1995) commemorates the Nazis' infamous book-burning of May 10, 1933, when students set alight 20,000 works by Jewish and humanist authors such as Freud, Heine, Thomas and Heinrich Mann. • **Bebelplatz** Ⓤ Friedrichstrasse, Französische Strasse Ⓢ Friedrichstrasse 🚌 100, 147, 200, TXL

St.-Hedwigs-Kathedrale (F3) The broad-domed Catholic cathedral was built by Friedrich the Great after 10,000 Catholics came to predominantly Protestant

Berlin following the Prussian conquest of Silesia in 1745. It was not finished until 1773. • Mon–Sat 10am–5pm; Sun 1–5pm ☏ 203 48 10 • Bebelplatz U Hausvogteiplatz, Französische Strasse 🚌 100, 147, 200, TXL

Staatsoper Unter den Linden (F3) On the east side of Bebelplatz, the national opera house (1743) was the first edifice of the Forum Fridericianum, the monumental complex with which Friedrich the Great wanted to express his personal attachment to the arts, scholarship and religious tolerance. Designed by Georg Wenzeslaus von Knobelsdorff in the style of a classical Palladian palazzo, the opera house staged the world premieres of Otto Nicolai's *Merry Wives of Windsor* in 1849 and Alban Berg's *Wozzeck* in 1925. • Guided tours in German some days of the week. Group tours available by reservation ☏ 20 35 44 38 • Unter den Linden 7 U Hausvogteiplatz, Französische Strasse, Friedrichstrasse S Friedrichstrasse 🚌 100, 200, TXL

Friedrich the Great Monument (F3) The Hohenzollerns' most illustrious king is honoured in the centre of the avenue with a masterly bronze equestrian statue by Christian Daniel Rauch, erected in 1851. Dozens of prominent Prussians of the philosopher-soldier's era are portrayed in sculpted relief on the pedestal. Critics deplore that the places of honour are reserved for military heroes and statesmen, while the playwright Gotthold Ephraim Lessing and the philosopher Emmanuel Kant are relegated to a lowly position beneath the horse's tail.

Humboldt University (F3) Berlin's first university (1810) completes the Forum Fridericianum on the north side of Unter den Linden. It was championed by Prussian statesman-scholar Wilhelm von Humboldt and housed in the palace built in 1766 for Friedrich's brother, Prince Heinrich. Illustrious alumni and teachers have included the brothers Grimm, philosophers Hegel and Schopenhauer, and scientists Einstein and Max Planck. Today the University has some 40,000 students. • Unter den Linden 6 U S Friedrichstrasse 🚌 100, 200, TXL

Neue Wache (F3) Next to the university, Karl Friedrich Schinkel's Doric-columned guardhouse, built for the Prussian Army in 1818, became a memorial for the Victims of War and the Rule of Force (Opfer von Krieg und Gewaltherrschaft) in 1993. The victims' monument in the hall is a controversial bronze Pietà of a mother cradling her dead son by Harald Haacke, based on a 40-cm miniature by sculptor Käthe Kollwitz and clumsily enlarged to four times the original size. • Daily 10am–6pm • Unter den Linden 4 U S Friedrichstrasse 🚌 100, 200, TXL

Zeughaus, Deutsches Historisches Museum (F–G3) Originally designed by Andreas Schlüter as an arsenal for the Prussian Army, the 17th-century Zeughaus is the new home of the German Historical Museum. The exhibitions trace the nation's tumultuous past in paintings, photographs and documentary films. At the rear of the grand baroque edifice is the striking modern Exhibition Hall by American architect I.M. Pei (2003), a triangular structure on four floors linked by a series of ramps and escalators and an elegant external cylindrical glass and steel tower encasing a spiral stairway. He also added a curved glass roof to the arsenal's inner courtyard, still adorned by Schlüter's brilliantly sculpted death-masks of warriors. Pei's building is used for temporary exhibitions. • Museum daily 10am–6pm ☎ 20 30 40 • Unter den Linden 2 U S Friedrichstrasse 🚌 100, 200, TXL

Prinzessinnenpalais (Opernpalais) (G3) On the south side of the avenue, the Prinzessinnenpalais (or Opernpalais), built in the 18th century for the Prussian princesses, was fancifully reconstructed in 1969. It is joined by bridge to the Kronprinzenpalais (Crown Princes' Palace), also restored and now a German government residence. The Prinzessinnenpalais houses several cafés and restaurants, including the very popular Operncafé and its open-air terrace. ☎ 20 26 83 • Unter den Linden 5 U S Friedrichstrasse 🚌 100, 200, TXL

Kommandantenhaus (map G3) The headquarters of the Prussian Commandery has been refurbished and since 2003 has been occupied by the Bertelsmann offices, a library, a bistro and bar. • Unter den Linden 1 U S Friedrichstrasse 🚌 100, 200, TXL

Schlossbrücke (G3) Linking Unter den Linden to what was once the royal palace, the castle bridge was built in 1821–24 to the design by Karl Friedrich

Schinkel. He also created its bronze reliefs of mythical sea creatures, but his designs for marble statues of military heroes were added later. The bridge joins the "mainland" Unter den Linden to the Spreeinsel in the middle of the Spree River where the fishermen of Cölln, Berlin's earliest community, had their homes.

Schlossplatz (G3) This vast square has been of enormous historical significance in city life. It was here in 1443 that Prince Elector Friedrich II von Hohenzollern built the first fortress. Known simply as the Berliner Schloss, it grew progressively in the 17th century until Andreas Schlüter's great façade, completed in 1706, made it the city's grandest baroque edifice. It was here, too, that the monarch, cheered by crowds on the square, saw his troops off to war in 1870 and 1914. In 1918, revolutionary leader Karl Liebknecht stood on the royal balcony to proclaim a bolshevik-style republic. The castle was gutted by fire in World War II and dismantled in 1951 by the East German regime as an unacceptable symbol of "monarchistic autocracy". It was replaced by the bronze-glass, steel and white marble Palast der Republik, home of the communist East German rubber-stamp parliament, closed in 1991 because of asbestos poisoning and then razed. It is planned to rebuild the castle, true to the original, from 2010. Until then, exhibitions of contemporary art are shown in a temporary gallery. • **Gallery daily 11am–6pm, Mon to 10pm** ☎ **20 45 36 50**

Berliner Dom (G3) With its great dome and four towers looming over the square's northeast corner, this gigantic neo-baroque cathedral was built in 1905 to give Kaiser Wilhelm II a German Protestant rival to St Peter's in Rome. It was to serve as the royal family's church and mausoleum—six Hohenzollerns are buried in the main church and another 94 in the crypt. The bright interior provides a colourful setting for theatre performances and concerts as well as church services. • **Mon–Sat 9am–8pm, Sun noon–8pm (Oct–Mar to 7pm)** ☎ **20 26 91 19** • **Am Lustgarten 1** 🆄 Alexanderplatz Ⓢ Hackescher Markt, Alexanderplatz 🚌 100, 200, TXL

Museumsinsel (F–G3) The northern end of the Spree island was developed as a museum complex back in 1830 and has now been undergoing extensive

restoration. Until the work of British architect David Chipperfield on the **Neues Museum** has been completed (autumn 2009), the bulk of the city's world-famous Egyptian collections, including their emblematic bust of Queen Nefertiti (1340 BC), is being housed in the Altes Museum. At the island's northernmost point, the neo-baroque **Bode-Museum**, dedicated to the national museums' revered director, Wilhelm von Bode, has been renovated and houses collections of sculpture, the Museum for Byzantine Art and on the second floor, the Münzkabinett (numismatic museum). • **Daily 10am-6pm, Thurs to 10pm. Alte Nationalgalerie closed Mon** ☎ 20 90 55 77 Ⓤ Ⓢ Friedrichstrasse, Hackescher Markt 🚌 100, 147, 200, TXL

Altes Museum (G3) The masterpiece of Schinkel (1830), the Altes Museum is one of the most important neoclassical monuments. The highlight is the rotunda supported by 20 Corinthian columns, modelled on Rome's Pantheon. Greek antiquities are exhibited on the ground floor, while the upper floor is devoted to the collections of the Egyptian Museum until March 2009; afterwards they will be removed to the Neues Museum.

Alte Nationalgalerie (map 2 G3) This museum displays major 19th-century works by German painters such as Schadow, Caspar David Friedrich, Böcklin, Feuerbach, Menzel and Lieberman, but also Cézanne, Manet and Rodin.

◀ *Nefertiti inspires awe in all who set eyes on her.*

Pergamon Museum (map 2 F–G3) Berlin's favourite museum groups three magnificent collections beneath its roof: the Antikensammlung (Greek and Roman antiquities); the Museum for Islamic Art, and the Middle East Museum. It is named after the ancient Greek Pergamon Altar, from the 2nd century BC. Dedicated to Zeus, the huge colonnaded marble altar was shipped in sections from Bergama in Turkish Anatolia to be installed here at the end of the 19th century. Sculpted friezes show Greek gods battling with giants. Archaeologists also reassembled the Processional Way and Ishtar Gate (562 BC) of the Babylonian king Nebuchadnezzar II. It depicts the lions of the goddess Ishtar striding along the blue and ochre glazed brick walls to the gate, which is adorned with divine bulls and dragons. The Roman Market Gateway of Miletus (AD 120), with its imposing arches and Ionic and Corinthian columns, completes the trio of monumental reconstructions. The museum is undergoing restoration but remains open for visits.

Oranienburger Strasse (F2) Trams and cars vie for space on this busy but relatively narrow shopping street, to which eastern Berlin's reviving Jewish community has returned, sharing the quarter with the more colourful elements of the city's "alternative" counter-culture—and prostitutes. At the corner of Tucholskystrasse, the splendid 19th-century glazed brick and terracotta Postfuhramt (Mail Coach Office) has been restored and now is used for prestigious photography exhibitions. At the east end of Oranienburger Strasse, a monumental Jugendstil (Art nouveau) façade beckons to a delightful group of courtyards, the **Hackesche Höfe**, between Rosenthaler- and Sophienstrasse. This classical piece of Berlin urban architecture has added to its original apartments and workshops a whole complex of art galleries, studios, restaurants, cafés, cabaret-theatre, cinemas and shops. The neighbourhood to the northeast is still known as **Scheunenviertel** (Barn District), from 17th-century grain storehouses subsequently used as workshops and tenements for Jewish refugees from Poland and Russia.

Museum Blindenwerkstatt Otto Weidt (G2) A poignant museum housed in Otto Weidt's Workshop for the Blind; from 1941 to 1943 the broom and brush manufacturer hid his Jewish blind and deaf employees in some of the rooms now used for the museum, to protect them from persecution and deportation. • Daily 10am–8pm ☎ 28 59 94 07 • Rosenthaler Strasse 39 Ⓤ Weinmeisterstrasse Ⓢ Hackescher Markt 🚋 M1, M4, M5

Neue Synagoge (F2) The gilded and glass Moorish-style domes of Germany's grandest synagogue (1866) give the street its landmark. It was protected from the Kristallnacht fires of 1938 by a brave Berlin policeman, but an Allied bomb hit it in 1943. The synagogue has been restored as a Centrum Judaicum. Marking the old Jewish cemetery on nearby Grosse Hamburger Strasse, razed by the Nazi Gestapo in 1943, is a gravestone for the community's famous 18th-century philosopher, Moses Mendelssohn. • Mar–Oct Sun–Mon 10am–8pm, Tues–Thurs 10am–6pm, Fri 10am–5pm (to 2pm Mar and Oct); Nov–Feb Sun–Thurs 10am–6pm, Fri 10am–2pm. Closed Sat and on Jewish holidays. ☎ 88 02 83 00 • Oranienburger Strasse 28/30 Ⓤ Oranienburger Tor Ⓢ Hackescher Markt 🚋 M1, M6

Tacheles – Internationales Kunsthaus (F2) A self-organized collective of artists preserved this old department store from demolition in 1990, first by occupying it and registering it as a historic landmark. Painted with large and colourful graffiti-style murals, and with modern sculptures in the courtyard, it has been transformed into an arts centre, with cinema, café, workshops, exhibition space, bars and nightclubs.
☎ 282 61 85 • Oranienburger Strasse 54–56a Ⓤ Oranienburger Tor
🚋 M1, M6, 12

The domes of the New Synagogue in Oranienburger Strasse.

WALKING TOUR: UNTER DEN LINDEN

The west end of Berlin's grandest avenue begins appropriately with the **Hotel Adlon**, grandest of the city's hostelries, 100 years old and still a favourite of statesmen and film stars. A right turn on **Wilhelmstrasse**, before World War II as synonymous with international diplomacy as Paris's Quai d'Orsay, leads to the new **British Embassy** (Britische Botschaft, 70–71) where two colourful "pop-architecture" elements jut out from an otherwise austere sandstone façade.

Turn right again on Behrenstrasse to Peter Eisenman's **Denkmal für die ermordeten Juden Europas** (Memorial to the Murdered Jews of Europe, 2005). Walk through its imposing maze of 2,711 concrete stelae before following Friedrich-Ebertstrasse to the **Brandenburger Tor**. In the northwest corner of Pariser Platz, emphasizing the gate's original symbolism of peace, is a public hall dedicated to silence, the **Raum der Stille**. The **French Embassy** (Französische Botschaft) is rebuilt on its old site, diplomatically ignoring the fact that Pariser Platz was named after the Prussian conquest of Paris in 1814. Cross over to continue east on **Unter den Linden** past the formidable Russian Embassy (Botschaft der Russischen Föderation), a Stalin commission of 1950, on your right.

Beyond the Komische Oper (entrance on Glinkastrasse), turn right on **Friedrichstrasse**, now the city's smartest shopping street. Among the many luxury German and Italian boutiques is the French department store **Galeries Lafayette**, naturally enough on the corner of Französische Strasse. This leads over to **Gendarmenmarkt**, where the two churches, Französischer and Deutscher Dom, and the Konzerthaus (formerly the Schauspielhaus theatre), are surrounded by pleasant tree-shaded cafés. Turn back north on Marktgrafenstrasse to **Bebelplatz**, the 18th-century Forum Fridericianum with the curved façade of the **Alte Bibliothek** (Old Library) and the **Staatsoper** (State Opera). Across Unter den Linden, beyond the statue of Friedrich II, is **Humboldt University**. At the east end of Bebelplatz, rest your tired feet on the terrace of the Operncafé in the **Opernpalais** (Prinzessinnenpalais).

UNTER DEN LINDEN 35

AROUND UNTER DEN LINDEN
Unter den Linden is once again Berlin's most prestigious avenue, lined with grand monuments, but with some great shopping and good cafés on its side streets.

Start:
Ⓢ Unter den Linden

Finish:
🚌 100, 200 Staatsoper

MUSIC IN BERLIN

A king's offering to a master

Music in Berlin had its auspicious beginnings in 1741 when Friedrich the Great took flute lessons, founded the Staatsoper (Opera House) on Unter den Linden and began composing music of his own. In 1747, he received Johann Sebastian Bach, whose son Carl Philipp Emanuel was the court musician. At his Sanssouci Palace, eager to show off his newly acquired gadget, an improved version of the recently invented pianoforte, the king presented his honoured guest with a theme which Bach undertook to transform into a fugue. The result was the great *Musikalisches Opfer* (Musical Offering).

Opera

In the 18th century, the works performed in Berlin's Royal Opera House were all Italian. German *Singspiele*, precursors of musical comedy, and French *opéra comique* attracted large audiences to private theatres. The "breakthrough" for serious German opera came in 1821 with the première of Carl Maria von Weber's Romantic *Der Freischütz*. Berlin-born composer Giacomo Meyerbeer (born Jakob Liebmann Beer) directed both Italian and German works at the Royal Opera, introducing Wagner to a sceptical Berlin public. Concert-goers were all middle class, as Berlin's aristocracy, unlike Vienna's, was hopelessly philistine.

At the turn of the 20th century, the Royal Opera House suffered from the prudery and conservatism of Kaiser Wilhelm II and his wife Augusta Victoria. Despite the fact that Richard Strauss was chief conductor and at the height of his fame, the empress, horrified by the pagan sensuality of his *Salomé*, insisted on a Star of Bethlehem rising at the end of the Berlin production to add a note of piety. Similarly, the Kaiser demanded cuts in *Der Rosenkavalier* to tone down the lechery of the opera's imperial chamberlain.

Berlin opera survived and thrived. In the 1920s, up to four opera houses were simultaneously active. At the Staatsoper, Erich Kleiber conducted premières of Alban Berg's *Wozzeck* and Leos Janacek's *Jenufa*, while Bruno

Walter was conducting at the Städtische Oper (Municipal Opera House) and Otto Klemperer at the Kroll. Today, the Deutsche Oper and Komische Oper perform miracles with tight budgets, while the Staatsoper remains the flagship, under Israeli conductor Daniel Barenboim.

Berlin Philharmonic Orchestra

Outshining a royal orchestra unable to sustain its illustrious beginnings under Felix Mendelssohn, the Berlin Philharmonic Orchestra was founded in 1882. Brahms and Richard Strauss both conducted, but it was director Hans von Bülow who instilled the discipline, attention to musical detail and the grand symphonic sweep of the repertoire's masterpieces that have become the Berlin Philharmonic's trademark. In the 1920s, Bruno Walter and Wilhelm Furtwängler built on the great tradition. Under Hitler, after the exile of Walter and other Jewish musicians, Furtwängler remained with the Philharmonic in his desperate belief that "the greatness of German music was the best and strongest negation of the spirit of Nazism". His subsequent successor, Herbert von Karajan, had no such compunctions, obtaining his Nazi Party card in 1933 and relying thereafter on his undisputable musical talents to gain recognition as one of the world's leading conductors. Today, the orchestra's reputation glows as brightly as ever under the direction of Liverpool-born Sir Simon Rattle. Its home since 1963 is the Philharmonie.

The Philharmonie was designed by Hans Scharoun.

ALEXANDERPLATZ

"Alex" to Berliners, the immense square has evolved from farmland to cattle market, military parade ground to modern traffic hub, attracting mass demonstrations in 1848, 1918 and again in November 1989—five days before the Wall came down. Today, it is a pedestrian zone around the railway station. Of its office blocks, some are architectural monuments like Peter Behrens' Alexander- and Berolinahaus (1932) on the south side of the square. Other characterless additions of the 1960s are being progressively demolished as part of plans to restore the square's central role in eastern Berlin life with a new group of skyscrapers. East of Alexanderplatz, the apartment buildings of Karl-Marx-Allee offer an intriguing glimpse of how the 1950s Stalinist architecture was given a facelift in the 1990s.

THE DISTRICT AT A GLANCE

SIGHTS

Architecture
Marienkirche............39
Nikolaikirche............41

Atmosphere
Nikolaiviertel ★........41

Entertainment
AquaDom
and Sea Life............39

Landmarks
Fernsehturm ★ 38
Berliner Rathaus......40

Museums
DDR Museum..........40
Knoblauchhaus 41

Ephraim-Palais 41
Märkisches
Museum ★ 41

WALKING TOUR 42

WINING AND DINING 101

Fernsehturm (G3) The 368-m (1,200-ft) Television Tower was inaugurated in 1969 as a bombastic counterpart to western Berlin's somewhat comic metal Funkturm, a 1920s "mini-Eiffel Tower" in Charlottenburg. The giant concrete needle pierces a steel-and-glass sphere two-thirds of the way up, with a revolving café and an observation deck with a terrific view. When the sun strikes the middle of the sphere, it reflects in the shape of a cross, which led the Berliners to give the tower the name "Pope's Revenge" as a jibe against the Communist

ALEXANDERPLATZ 39

The famous Fernsehturm and buildings along the Spree, viewed from the Märkisches Ufer.

government. • March–Oct daily 9am–midnight Nov–Feb daily 10am–midnight ☎ 242 33 33 • Panoramastrasse 1a U S Alexanderplatz Tram M2, M4, M5, M6 BUS 200, 248, M48, TXL

Marienkirche (G3) A bit out of the way, not far from the TV tower, this slender 13th-century Gothic structure is one of Berlin's oldest parish churches. The most famous work inside the church is the 15th-century *Totentanz* (Dance of Death) frieze on the north aisle; also of interest are the marble pulpit (1703) by Andreas Schlüter and the organ (1721) by Joachim Wagner. • Oct–Mar 10am–6pm; Apr–Sept 10am–9pm; Sat and Sun no admission during services ☎ 242 44 67 • Karl-Liebknecht-Strasse 8 U S Alexanderplatz Tram M2, M4, M5, M6 BUS 200, 248, M48, TXL

AquaDom and Sea Life (G3) The exotic underwater world is presented in 30 natural fresh- and seawater aquariums—but the main attraction is a ride in a transparent elevator through a cylindrical acrylic glass aquarium, 25 m high and the largest in the world. It contains 2,600 fish of 56 species, which are fed by two full-time divers. • Daily 10am–7pm, last entry 6pm ☏ 99 28 00 • Spandauer Strasse 3 Ⓤ Ⓢ Alexanderplatz Tram M4, M5, M6 Bus 200, 248, M48, TXL

DDR Museum (G3) Opened in 2006, this unusual museum stands directly opposite the cathedral on the other side of the Spree, and plunges visitors into the life and times of East Berlin by means of interactive displays. You can see a typical family apartment, climb aboard a Trabant or try out the Stasi's espionage material. • Sun–Fri 10am–8pm, Sat 10am–10pm ☏ 847 123 731 • Karl-Liebknecht-Strasse 1 Ⓤ Ⓢ Alexanderplatz Tram M4, M5, M6 Bus 200, 248, M48, TXL

Berliner Rathaus (G3) Southwest of the Fernsehturm, the imposing Rotes Rathaus (Red Town Hall), earned its popular nickname from its red brick. The building, dating from 1869, found a new purpose in 1991 as residence of the city mayor in office. • Mon–Fri 9am–6pm (except during official events) ☏ 902 60 • Rathausstrasse 15 Ⓤ Klosterstrasse, Alexanderplatz Ⓢ Alexanderplatz Tram M2, M4, M5, M6 Bus 248, M48

◀ *The twin spires of Nikolaikirche, heart of the Nikolaiviertel.*

ALEXANDERPLATZ 41

Nikolaiviertel (G3) One of the more popular urban achievements of the East German authorities was the reconstruction of the medieval neighbourhood between the town hall and the Mühlendamm embankment. Picturesque restaurants and wine-bars cluster around the twin-steepled Gothic parish church.

Nikolaikirche (G3) Closed till mid 2009 for extensive renovation. Built around 1230, the church—one of the most important religious buildings in Berlin, as well as being the oldest—was completely destroyed in 1945. After its reconstruction in 1987 it has served as a department of the Märkisches Museum. ☎ 24 00 21 62 • Nikolaikirchplatz **U** Klosterstrasse, Alexanderplatz **S** Alexanderplatz 🚋 M2, M4, M5, M6 🚌 248, M48

Knoblauchhaus (map 2 G3) Nothing to do with garlic *(Knoblauch)*, this baroque townhouse was the home, for 170 years, of the cultivated Knoblauch family, who traded in silk. Built in 1761, the building was given a neoclassic façade in 1806. It once once welcomed illustrious guests such as Mendelssohn and Lessing. Today it is a museum documenting generations of Knoblauchs in an exhibition entitled "Bourgeois life in Biedermeier days". • Tues, Thurs–Sun 10am–6pm, Wed noon–8pm ☎ 24 00 21 62 • Poststrasse 23 **U** Klosterstrasse, Alexanderplatz **S** Alexanderplatz 🚋 M2, M4, M5, M6 🚌 248, M48

Ephraim-Palais (G3) In the 18th-century rococo home of court banker Veitel Heine Ephraim, this museum displays the city's Graphische Sammlung, a collection of some 90,000 drawings and etchings, and presents changing exhibitions pertaining to Berlin's art and history. • Tues, Thurs–Sun 10am–6pm, Wed noon–8pm ☎ 24 00 21 21 • Poststrasse 16 **U** Klosterstrasse, Alexanderplatz **S** Alexanderplatz 🚋 M2, M4, M5, M6 🚌 248, M48

Märkisches Museum (H4) On the river's south bank, this museum was founded in 1874 and is a compendium of all the architectural styles of Brandenburg. Today it is the headquarters of the Berlin City Museum. The collections give insight into the cultural history of Berlin and Brandenburg from early times to the 20th century. • Tues, Thurs, Sun 10am–6pm, Wed noon–8pm, Fri, Sat 2–10pm ☎ 30 86 60 • Am Köllnischen Park 5 **U** Märkisches Museum, Jannowitzbrücke **S** Jannowitzbrücke 🚌 147

WALKING TOUR: ALEXANDERPLATZ

From **Alexanderplatz** and its huge **Fernsehturm**, walk past the red-brick clocktower of the Berliner or **Rotes Rathaus**, once again seat of the city's mayor. From Spandauer Strasse, turn back north on Grunerstrasse to Klosterstrasse and the ruin of the 13th-century Franciscan **Klosterkirche**, originally Berlin's most important Gothic church and now a picturesque setting for open-air concerts and art exhibitions. Behind the church, Littenstrasse leads to the narrow Waisenstrasse and remains of the medieval **Stadtmauer** (city wall), serving in some places as a rear wall for the street's 16th- and 17th-century houses. Most noteworthy of these is the old—some say the city's oldest—tavern, **Zur letzten Instanz** (Court of Final Appeal, alluding to the nearby district courthouse on Littenstrasse, Amtsgericht Mitte—verdict: pretty good).

Double back via Parochialstrasse to Klosterstrasse, and look in at the **Parochialkirche**, the parish church destroyed in 1944 and partially rebuilt from 1991 to 2004; its raw stonework a reminder of the war. Two buildings further along, **Warenhaus Tietz,** former head office of the august Berlin department store chain "aryanized" by the Nazis in the 1930s and now elegantly refurbished as an office building. Continue south to the **Dutch Embassy** (Niederländische Botschaft, 2001 by Holland's top architect Rem Koolhaas) intentionally built on the waterfront to make embassy staff feel more at home. Turn right on Rolandufer along the Spree to the river's first bridge, the **Mühlendammbrücke**, and the rococo **Ephraim-Palais**, displaying the Graphische Sammlung of the municipal museum.

On the bridge (by the north-bound bus-stop) take the steps down to the **Fischerinsel**, the island park once the home of Berlin's first inhabitants and now a pleasant place for a summer siesta or picnic. From the east end of the island, cross the Inselbrücke to the **Märkisches Museum** on the Spree's south bank. Take the Märkisches Ufer past the sparkling mirror façade of the massive new **Chinese Embassy** (Chinesische Botschaft) near the Jannowitzbrücke (railway bridge). Opposite the embassy is one of the town's best Chinese restaurants, the **Ming Dynastie** (Brückenstrasse 6), something of a luxury canteen for the diplomats.

ALEXANDERPLATZ 43

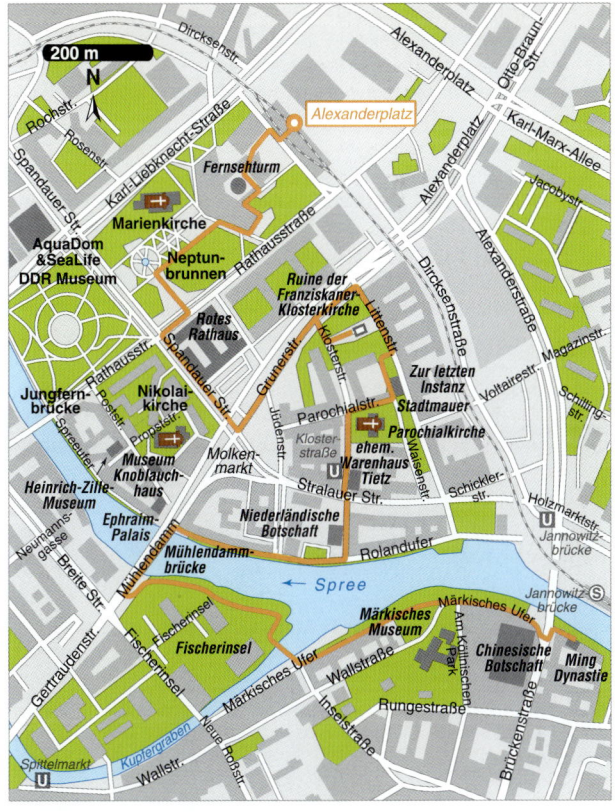

FROM "ALEX" AROUND THE SPREEINSEL
Stroll from the hub of the city's modern historic gatherings on the "Alex" around the original 11th-century island settlement in the middle of the River Spree.

Start: 🇺 🇸 Alexanderplatz **Finish:** 🇺 🇸 Jannowitzbrücke

AN EVER-CHANGING SKYLINE

Over the two decades since the Wall came down, visitors could easily get the impression that Berlin is a perennial building site. Re-creating a single national capital out of the city's Western and Eastern sectors launched a feverish construction boom without equal in the modern world. At the height of the construction activity, the building sites themselves, particularly on and around Potsdamer Platz, became a tourist attraction—a veritable ballet, floodlit at night, of gracefully soaring cranes, swinging wrecking-balls and trundling bulldozers. Things have calmed down a bit now, but there is still plenty of heavy machinery around the northeast corner of the Tiergarten, on Schlossplatz and the venerable buildings on Museumsinsel, with their seemingly never-ending makeovers.

In fact, Berlin has always undergone drastic changes throughout its turbulent history, but never more so than in the 20th century when it was subjected to ideologically-driven construction—and destruction—by Nazi and Communist dictatorships as well as the devastation of World War II bombs. Today's urban landscape reflects these monumental ups and downs in dramatic juxtapositions of buildings old and new, accidentally or deliberately thrust together with effects that are variously poignant, grotesque, beautiful, charming and sometimes even comical.

Lesson in humility

Nothing subtle about the gesture the East German Communist dictatorship made in 1969 when it planted the gigantic **Fernsehturm** (Television Tower) on the site of medieval Berlin's beginnings south of Alexanderplatz. This was to be the triumphant emblem of the German Democratic Republic's capital. Today, its location near the splendid dignity of the 13th-century red-brick Gothic **Marienkirche** reminds us that grandeur is not just a matter of dimension.

Declaration of intent

The best known of Berlin's architectural juxtapositions came about as a quite conscious decision. The bombed-out ruin of the 19th-century **Kaiser-Wilhelm-Gedächtnis-Kirche** was preserved, broken steeple and all, to be flanked now by a modern hexagonal belltower and octagonal chapel. Standing on Breitscheidplatz at the eastern entrance to the Kurfürstendamm, the structures were conceived in 1961—at the West Berliners' own popular demand—to recall the catastrophe of war while renewing the city's faith in its present and future.

Then and now
At the **Olympiastadion**, the juxtaposition is not of two buildings but of two memories. Adolf Hitler's bombastic monumental stadium was built for the infamous Olympic Games of 1936 and the saluting parades through the Marathon Gate. In preparation for Berlin's hosting of the 2006 football World Cup, the oval stadium has been given an elegant new glass and steel roof. To counter the ponderous impact of the original massive stone-clad concrete structure, everything has been done to make the place light and airy. But it is still the Olympiastadion and in this case, the weight of history may resist all attempts at a facelift.

"Hey! I'm still here."
In the reconstruction following German unification in 1990, **Potsdamer Platz** became the biggest building site of them all, covering a total area of 48 hectares. What had been a teeming, tumultuous hub of city life in the heyday of Berlin's Roaring Twenties was reduced to a bleak, flat wasteland. Somehow, one building had survived, the **Weinhaus Huth** tavern, erected there in 1910. This quaint domed relic of Wilhelminian Germany is back in business today, surrounded and dwarfed by the soaring towers of such international architectural giants as Renzo Piano, Helmut Jahn and Richard Rogers.

Two Realities

The two starkly contrasting buildings comprising the **Jüdisches Museum** on Lindenstrasse may seem like a visual expression of the Jewish destiny in Berlin. The entrance to the museum is through Philippe Gerlach's graceful 18th-century baroque **Kammergericht** (courthouse), built in the enlightened era of Friedrich the Great when Jewish philosopher Moses Mendelssohn was an honoured member of the Berlin community. It leads to the museum's exhibitions in Daniel Libeskind's formidable angular concrete structure evoking the 20th century's fractured Star of David.

Window on Democracy

Sometimes old and new come happily together in the same building. After the **Reichstag** was built in 1894, Kaiser Wilhelm II opposed the idea of inscribing *Dem deutschen Volk* (To the German People) on the façade, but he was too preoccupied with World War I to stop it being added in 1916. It is safe to say he would not have liked the translucent glass dome with which British architect Norman Foster crowned it in 1999. Now the German people, in their droves, cheerfully take daily possession of their parliament by climbing up into the dome overlooking the debating chamber *(Plenarsaal)*.

POTSDAMER PLATZ

Potsdamer Platz is back. Fanning out from the old square to the new Marlene-Dietrich-Platz, the area is bustling once more with ultra-modern cinemas, hotels, casino, shopping mall, restaurants, apartments and office blocks.

THE DISTRICT AT A GLANCE

SIGHTS	Museums	Viewpoint
	Museum für Film und Fernsehen 49	Hi-Flyer 49
Architecture		
Potsdamer Platz ★ ...48	Museum für Kommunikation........50	**WALKING TOUR** 52
Anhalter Bahnhof....51		
Memorial		**WINING AND DINING** 102
Topographie des Terrors 50	Martin-Gropius-Bau ★ 50	

Potsdamer Platz (E4) From the day the city's first railway station opened here in 1838, what had been a quiet crossroads on the way to Potsdam grew into a sprawling "town within a town", the epicentre of Berlin's metropolitan tumult. Europe's busiest city square in the 1920s—registering more traffic than London's Marble Arch or Paris's Place de la Concorde—became Europe's largest construction site in the 1990s. Renowned architects came from all over the world to fill the vast 48-ha (120-acre) wasteland left by wartime bombs and the neglect of the Wall years. The main thoroughfare of this new district is Neue Potsdamer Strasse, separating the Daimler-Areal from the Sony Center, and ending at Potsdamer Platz. Italy's Renzo Piano designed the tall **debis-Haus** for the Quartier Daimler-Chrysler, with a slim, 106-m-high tower topped by a gleaming green cube. Neighbouring buildings were designed by local architect Hans Kollhoff and the Japanese Arata Isozaki. From the top of the Panoramapunkt, 96 m (118 ft) high up in the Kohlhoff-Tower, you get a good view of this spectacular urban revival. Chicago's Helmut Jahn built the **Sony Center** entertain-

A shimmering Balloon Flower *by Jeff Koons reflects Marlene-Dietrich-Platz.*

ment complex beneath a fibre-glass flat-topped pyramid recalling the Japanese manufacturer's beloved Mount Fuji. Only two buildings survived World War II: **Weinhaus Huth**, with three modern food courts, and a part of the grand old Esplanade hotel appropriated for the Sony Center complex.

Museum für Film und Fernsehen (E4) A glimpse into the history of the German film industry, from the pioneering years and silent films to contemporary cinema. Several rooms are devoted to Marlene Dietrich. The installation of a new TV museum has turned the showcase of the German cinematheque into a comprehensive house of moving images. There is also a library, a café and a boutique. • Daily (except Mon) 10am–6pm, Thurs to 8pm ☎ 300 90 30 • Potsdamer Strasse 2 **U** **S** Potsdamer Platz Tram Bus M48, 200

Hi-Flyer (F4) To see the city from on high, take a levitating trip in this enormous helium balloon—one of the biggest in the world—that glides silently

above the rooftops to an altitude of 150 m. It is firmly attached by a cable which pulls you back to the ground again. • **Summer: Sun–Thurs 10am–10pm, Fri, Sat 10am–0.30am; winter: Sun–Thurs 11am–6pm, Fri, Sat 11am–7pm. Weather information** ☎ 22 66 77 811 • Corner Wilhelmstrasse and Zimmerstrasse 🅄 Mohrenstrasse, Kochstrasse 🚌 200, M29, M48

Museum für Kommunikation (F4) Three robots greet visitors in the glass-covered courtyard of the world's oldest post office museum. The exhibits cover communications from their beginnings to modern times. There is also a fascinating collection of postage stamps, including a Blue Mauritius. • **Tues–Fri 9am–5pm, Sat, Sun 10am–6pm** ☎ 20 29 40 • Leipziger Strasse 16 🅄 Mohrenstrasse, Stadtmitte 🚌 M48, 200

Topographie des Terrors (F4) Over the remains of the Nazi Gestapo headquarters, an open-air exhibition documents how, in the former Prinz-Albrecht Hotel, Heinrich Himmler's secret police imprisoned, tortured and murdered its political and "racial" enemies. A permanent documentation centre will be completed by mid 2010. • **Daily Oct–Apr 10am–6 pm or till dusk; May–Sept 10am–8pm** ☎ 25 45 09 50 • Niederkirchnerstrasse 8 🅄 Potsdamer Platz, Kochstrasse 🅢 Anhalter Bahnhof, Potsdamer Platz 🚌 M29, M41

Martin-Gropius-Bau (E–F 4–5) This lovingly restored 19th-century building was designed in neo-Renaissance style by the great-uncle of Bauhaus master Walter Gropius. It stages first-rate temporary exhibitions of art, sculpture, archaeology, photography and cultural history. Pleasant café and bookshop. • **Daily (except Tues) 10am–8pm** ☎ 25 48 60 • Niederkirchnerstrasse 7 🅄 Potsdamer Platz 🅢 Anhalter Bahnhof, Potsdamer Platz 🚌 M29, M41

Anhalter Bahnhof (F5) Further south, another eloquent ruin can be seen, the arcades of the yellow-brick neo-Renaissance façade of what was once the city's most glamorous railway station. It was from here, after 1933, that some of Germany's most famous people went into exile: Einstein, Grosz, Brecht and Kurt Weill. Designed by Franz Schwechten, the station was closed down and demolished in 1952. • **Askanischer Platz** Ⓢ **Anhalter Bahnhof** 🚍 **M29, M41**

FALLING IN LOVE AGAIN

Beloved and resented, Marlene Dietrich was Germany's first film actress to make it big in Hollywood. Born in 1901, Marie Magdalene was the daughter of a police officer, in what was then the Berlin suburb of Schöneberg. Aged 11, she already asserted an independent spirit by changing her name to Marlene. She abandoned studies as a violinist in favour of the theatre, training in 1921 under the great Max Reinhardt. After a dozen small parts in silent films, she caught the attention of director Josef von Sternberg for the role as cabaret singer and dancer Lola in *The Blue Angel* (1930). Filmed in English and German, it made her an instant world star, both for her seductive acting and her singing—most notably *Falling In Love Again*. She emigrated with Sternberg to Hollywood in the 1930s and worked there with Alfred Hitchcock, Ernst Lubitsch, Orson Welles and Billy Wilder. At the height of her fame, she turned down a huge offer from Josef Goebbels to return to work in Nazi Germany, became an American citizen and an immensely popular entertainer with American troops fighting in Europe. For this, she was condemned by a small but vocal minority of Germans as a "traitor to the fatherland" when she returned to sing there in 1960. She died in her Paris home in 1992, but was buried beside her mother in a Berlin cemetery and given due civic honours when Marlene-Dietrich-Platz was inaugurated in the Potsdamer Platz entertainment district.

WALKING TOUR: POTSDAMER PLATZ

Named after one of the most celebrated theatre and film actresses of the Weimar Republic's Golden Twenties, the long grassy slopes of the **Tilla-Durieux-Park** lead to the resurrected bustling entertainment district of Potsdamer Platz where she made her name. On the right, the park is flanked on Gabriele-Tergit Promenade by the red-brick office blocks of the **Park Kolonnaden**, culminating in a gracefully curved steel and glass apartment building like the engine of a train arriving at the gleaming new towers on **Potsdamer Platz**. Turn right on Stresemannstrasse to the **IBA-Hochhaus (Wohnhof)** building (No. 109) leaning forward over the corner of Dessauer Strasse. With its façade of bronze metal and glass, this apartment house was designed in 1993 by avant-garde Baghdad-born British woman architect Zaha Hadid.

Backtrack to Niederkirchnerstrasse, leading to the imposing red-brick **Martin-Gropius-Bau**, a museum hosting an eclectic variety of first-rate modern exhibitions. Its entrance has been restored to the north side portico now that nearby graffiti-covered remains of the **Berlin Wall** *(Mauerreste)* are all that can be seen here of the old East-West Berlin border. Behind the Wall can be seen another relic of Germany's totalitarian past, bleak ruins of the Nazi Gestapo headquarters transformed into a open-air exhibit, **"Topographie des Terrors"**.

At the far end of the exhibit, turn right into Wilhelmstrasse, where signs highlight some of the important ministries of Prussia and the German Reich that lined the street in 1945. Take Anhalterstrasse to get back to Stresemannstrasse and turn left to another, more graceful relic, the neo-Renaissance yellow-brick façade of one of the city's grandest railway stations, the **Anhalter Bahnhof**. Its railway tracks have been replaced by a football field and, at the far end, the white tent-shaped wooden roof of the **Tempodrom** hall, staging musical comedies and pop concerts. Hallesche Strasse leads back through another wooded park to Stresemannstrasse and, on the right, the red-flagged **Willy-Brandt-Haus** (1996), headquarters of Germany's Social Democratic Party (SPD), named after its long-time leader, Mayor of West Berlin and West German Chancellor. His bust can be seen in the entrance hall.

POTSDAMER PLATZ 53

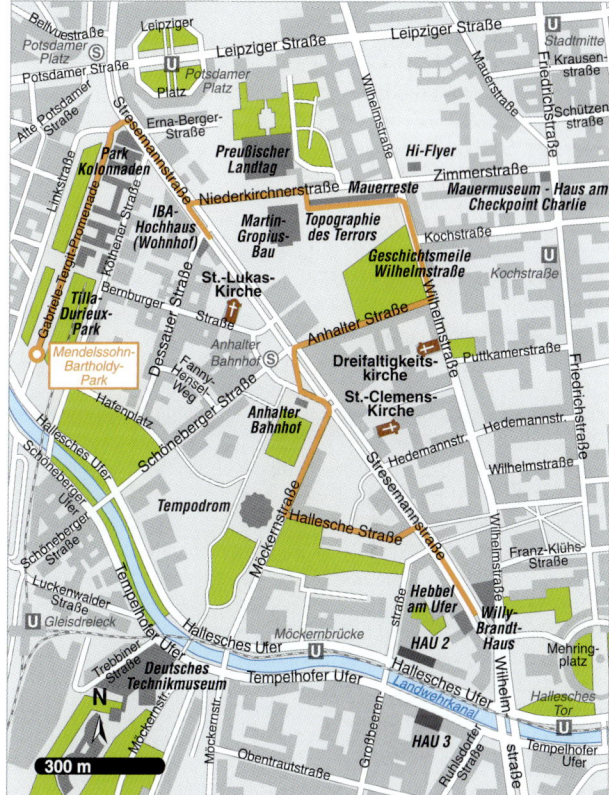

BRANCHING OUT FROM POTSDAMER PLATZ
This neighbourhood at the old border between East and West Berlin combines some interesting modern architecture with grim reminders of the recent past.

Start: U Mendelssohn-Bartholdy-Park   **Finish:** U Hallesches Tor

REMEMBERING THE WALL

The Wall that split Berlin in half from 1961 to to 1989 was officially called the Antifaschistischer Schutzwall (antifascisct protective rampart) by the East German government and the Wall of Shame in the West. It has now almost completely disappeared. After its chaotic destruction, when lumps of it were sold as souvenirs, a few remaining segments were declared a historic monument. These vestiges, along with commemorative monuments and museums devoted to the Wall, are the most significant symbol of the division of Germany. The longest stretches are on **Niederkirchnerstrasse**, east of the Martin-Gropius-Bau (Ⓤ Ⓢ Potsdamer Platz), near the **Invalidenfriedhof** (Ⓤ Zinnowitzer Strasse) and in the **Mauerpark** (Wall Park, Ⓤ Eberswalder Strasse). Elsewhere in the city, a double row of cobblestones marks the **former frontier**, which stretched for 45 km. A permanent exhibition, the **Berlin Wall History Mile** (Geschichtsmeile Berliner Mauer) consists of 30 information panels set at various points along the site of the wall, commemorating events that took place at those spots. In 2006, the **Wall Trail** (Berliner Mauerweg) opened: this 160 km (100 mile) route traces the former frontier between West Berlin and East Germany and is dotted with information panels and maps. At several points along the way you can hire a multimedia MauerGuide including a GPS navigator. Several activities are organized for the 20th anniversary of the fall of the Wall in 2009 (www.mauerfall09.de).

East Side Gallery (map 1 I4–J5) The longest remaining section of the wall stretches over 1.3 km between the Ostbahnhof and the Oberbaumbrücke. In the atmosphere of euphoria that reigned from 1989 to 1990, artists came from the world over to paint its untouched east side. The 106 paintings did not survive erosion, vandalism and graffiti, and many are now being restored for the second time. • Mühlenstraße, Friedrichshain Ⓤ Warschauer Strasse Ⓢ Warschauer Strasse, Ostbahnhof 🚋 M10, M13 🚌 140, 147, 240

Checkpoint Charlie (F4) From 1961 to 1989, this was one of the most famous focal points of the Cold War. Between Kochstrasse and Zimmerstrasse, the US Army manned a checkpoint at the border crossing between West and East Berlin. On the other side, East German border guards were delegated by their Soviet masters to control traffic and watch out for fugitives, while customs officials checked papers and personal belongings. Around the customs sheds was a vast floodlit no-man's-land with tank-traps, obstacles to slow down traffic and watchtowers for armed guards. Today, the Friedrichstrasse crossing is marked only by its old sign: "You Are Leaving the American Sector", and two large photos in the middle of the road—a Soviet soldier facing south and an American soldier facing north. Ⓤ Kochstrasse, Stadtmitte

Mauermuseum – Haus am Checkpoint Charlie (F4) The small and impressive private Wall Museum documents life in the divided city and recounts by use of original artefacts some of the successful attempts at escape under or over the Wall—and the unfortunate ones. A separate exhibition illustrates the world-wide non-violent struggle for human rights. • Daily 9am–10pm ☎ 253 72 50 • Friedrichstrasse 43–45 Ⓤ Kochstrasse, Stadtmitte

Parlament der Bäume/Gedenkort Weisse Kreuze (E3) On the former border at Schiffbauerdamm, the "Parliament of Trees" combines segments of the Wall, trees, photographs and texts, commemorating those who lost their lives at the Wall. Opposite on Reichstagufer stands a collection of white crosses that had originally been set up at every spot where a fugitive was killed. • Schiffbauerdamm/Reichstagufer Ⓢ Unter den Linden 🚌 100, 147, M85, TXL

Gedenkstätte Berliner Mauer (F1) The central memorial site for the victims of the Communist regime stands at a particularly dramatic place, for on Bernauer Strasse the Wall passed straight through the houses. Windows and doors were blocked up to prevent any escape, yet it was here that there were the most attempts. The memorial comprises a section of the Wall rebuilt on its original site, enhanced by artistic means, a documentation centre and the oval Chapel of Reconciliation, built on rammed earth with a framework of wooden staves, on the site of the earlier Church of the Reconciliation Parish of 1894, blown up in 1985 by the East German government. An information pavilion will be completed for the 50th anniversary of the construction of the Wall, August 13, 2011. • Daily except Mon, Apr–Oct 10am–6pm, Nov–Mar 10am–5pm ☎ 464 10 30 • Bernauer Strasse 111 Ⓤ Bernauer Strasse Ⓢ Nordbahnhof 🚋 M8, M10, 12 🚌 245, 247

TIERGARTEN

The Tiergarten, a pleasant park, has given its name to the whole neighbourhood between Mitte and Charlottenburg. The "Animal Garden" was a forest where the Hohenzollern kings hunted for deer and wild boar. Today, it is a popular venue for picnics, particularly for Turkish barbecues, and rock concerts and for boating on its ponds. The park is split by the broad, straight Strasse des 17. Juni (date of an East German workers' uprising in 1953). At weekends a flea market and crafts market are held in front of the S-Bahn Tiergarten station. In the southeast of the park is the Kulturforum and its museums of European art.

THE DISTRICT AT A GLANCE

SIGHTS

Architecture
Kulturforum.............56
Philharmonie ★ 57
St.-Matthäus-Kirche 59
Band des Bundes ★ .63

Entertainment
Zoologischer Garten 60
Haus der Kulturen der Welt.................60

Landmarks
Siegessäule 60
Reichstag ★ 60
Bundeskanzleramt...63

Memorial
Gedenkstätte Deutscher Widerstand 59

Museums
Musikinstrumenten-Museum 57
Gemäldegalerie ★ ..58
Kunstgewerbemuseum..................58

Kupferstichkabinett .58
Neue Nationalgalerie ★ 58
Bauhaus Archiv/ Museum für Gestaltung.............59
Hamburger Bahnhof – Museum für Gegenwart ★ 63

WALKING TOUR 64

WINING AND DINING 103

Kulturforum (D–E4) The area between Potsdamer Platz and the Landwehr canal was left as a wasteland after World War II. Since the 1960s it has been completely transformed into a cultural complex designed by architects such as Mies van der Rohe, Hans Scharoun and Hilmer & Sattler. With museums, concert halls, libraries and institutes, it has become one of the cultural highlights

The Marie-Elisabeth-Lüders-Haus is part of the Band des Bundes, the new parliament buildings along the Spree.

of Berlin. 🆄 Potsdamer Platz, Mendelssohn-Bartholdy-Park 🆂 Potsdamer Platz 🚌 200, M29, M41, M48, M85

Philharmonie (E4) Hans Scharoun, who masterminded the Kulturforum's original concept, built this tent-like home for the Berlin Philharmonic Orchestra in keeping with his taste for free-form structure. Working closely with Herbert von Karajan, he gave the orchestra awesome acoustics. The building is flanked by the Kammermusiksaal (Chamber Music Hall), also called the Kleine Philharmonie. • Tours daily at 1pm ☎ 25 48 80 • Herbert-von-Karajan-Strasse 1

Musikinstrumenten-Museum (E4) Comprehensive collections of historic musical instruments from the 16th to 20th centuries, including Europe's biggest theatre organ. You can play some of the instruments yourself in the studio, or watch a demonstration of keyboard instruments. • Tues, Wed, Fri 9am–5pm, Thurs 9am–10pm, Sat, Sun 10am–5pm ☎ 25 48 11 78 • Ben-Gurion-Strasse

Gemäldegalerie (D4) At the heart of the Tiergarten's Kulturforum complex, this museum presents one of the world's finest collections of European painting, from the Middle Ages to the 18th century. After 50 years of Cold War separation, the collections from the Museumsinsel in the east and Dahlem in the west have been reunited in this wonderful setting. Superb lighting enhances the paintings. The highlights include German: Schongauer, Altdorfer, Dürer and Cranach; Dutch and Flemish: Van Eyck, Memling, Brueghel, Rubens, Van Dyck, Rembrandt and Vermeer; Italian: Giotto, Botticelli, Raphael, Giorgione and Caravaggio; French: Georges de la Tour, Poussin and Watteau; Spanish: Velázquez and Zurbarán; English: Reynolds and Gainsborough. • **Daily except Mon 10am–6pm (Thurs 10am–10pm)** ☎ 266 29 51 • Matthäikirchplatz

Kunstgewerbemuseum (E4) The Applied Arts Museum displays an interesting collection of European arts and crafts from the Middle Ages to the present. Among the main attractions are the Guelf treasure with gold ornaments forged in Brunswick in the 11th to 15th centuries, and the silver treasure of the Lüneburg city council (15th–16th centuries). • **Tues–Fri 10am–6pm, Sat, Sun 11am–6pm** ☎ 266 29 02 • Matthäikirchplatz

Kupferstichkabinett (D4) The Museum of Prints and Drawings owns around 110,000 watercolours, pastels, oil sketches and drawings as well as 550,000 prints, including works by Botticelli, Dürer, Rembrandt, Menzel, Picasso and Warhol—one of the most important collections in the world. • **Tues–Fri 10am–6pm, Sat, Sun 11am–6pm** ☎ 266 29 51 • Matthäikirchplatz

Neue Nationalgalerie (E4) The striking four-square black steel and glass gallery for modern sculpture and painting is a late work (1968) of Bauhaus architect Ludwig Mies van der Rohe. The gallery stages prestigious temporary exhibitions on the ground floor, with its permanent collection on the lower level. There are major works by Edvard Munch, Kokoschka and Picasso, Kirchner, Klee, Feiniger and Dix. Sculpture on the outside terrace presents works by Ernst, Giacometti, Moore, Picasso and Calder. • **Tues, Wed, Fri 10am–6pm, Thurs 10am–10pm, Sat, Sun 11am–6pm. The permanent collection is sometimes closed when temporary exhibitions are being installed.** ☎ 266 29 51 • Potsdamer Strasse 50

St.-Matthäus-Kirche (E4) The simple little neo-Romanesque church (1846) behind the Neue Nationalgalerie stands in piquant contrast to the forum's modern architecture. It was damaged during World War II but was restored in the 1960s. Apart from the evangelical church services, the church is also used for cultural exhibitions and is an integral part of the Kulturforum complex. • **Daily except Mon noon–6pm** ☎ 262 12 02 • Matthäikirchplatz

Gedenkstätte Deutscher Widerstand (D4) The German Resistance Memorial Centre is located at the historic site of the attempted coup of July 20, 1944, in the Bendler Block, which has been the office of the German Federal Ministry of Defense since 1993. The permanent exhibition documents the struggle against National Socialism, showing how resistance was formed and developed from 1933 to 1945. • **Mon–Wed, Fri 9am–6pm, Thurs 9am–8pm, Sat, Sun 10am–6pm. Free admission** ☎ 26 99 50 00 • Stauffenbergstrasse 13–14 Ⓤ Kurfürstenstrasse, Potsdamer Platz Ⓢ Potsdamer Platz 🚌 M29, M48, 200

Bauhaus-Archiv/Museum für Gestaltung (D5) For the archives and exhibition halls of the historic Bauhaus design school, which functioned from 1919 to 1933, its founder Walter Gropius designed the building completed in 1978, nine years after his death. On a bank of the Landwehr canal, it houses original Bauhaus furniture, textiles, architectural models, sculpture, paintings, fabrics and other art works, and is the biggest collection of Bauhaus design in the world. Temporary exhibitions are held.

MIES

Bauhaus architect Ludwig Mies Van der Rohe had mixed feelings about Berlin. He had made his name with the German Pavilion for Barcelona Expo 1929, but his other masterpieces were designed in the US. Only reluctantly did he respond to Berlin's request that he build the elegant Neue Nationalgalerie for the Kulturforum, and even then it's believed to be based on drawings he had made for a factory in Cuba. When Bauhaus colleagues like Walter Gropius and Marcel Breuer emigrated to the US in 1933, Mies stayed behind and did not leave till 1937, when he saw that Hitler had too many architectural ideas of his own for the master builder to find any satisfying work in the Third Reich.

• Daily except Tues 10am–5pm ☎ 254 00 20 • Klingelhöferstrasse 14 Ⓤ Nollendorfplatz 🚌 100, 106, 187, M29

Zoologischer Garten (B4–C5) The entrance to the zoo, which opened in 1884, is through a pagoda-roofed Elephant Gate. Berlin's zoo is one of the biggest in the world. Among the 19,000 animals on view are Indian and African elephants, pandas, rhinoceros and crocodiles. The polar bear Knut, born here on December 5, 2006, is its star attraction. • **Mid Mar–mid Oct 9am–6.30pm, rest of year 9am–5pm** ☎ 25 40 10 • Hardenbergplatz 8; Budapester Strasse 32/34 Ⓤ Ⓢ Zoologischer Garten 🚌 100, 109, 110, 145, 200, 245, 249, M45, M46, M49, X9, X10, X34

Siegessäule (C3) Soaring above the Grosser Stern traffic circle at the centre of the Tiergarten, this Victory Column (1873) celebrates Prussian victories over Denmark in 1864, Austria in 1866 and France in 1871. Beneath the gilded statue of Winged Victory is an observation platform reached by a spiral staircase of 285 steps. On the north side of the traffic circle are statues of Chancellor Bismarck, Fieldmarshal Moltke and War Minister Roon. • **Apr–Oct Mon–Fri 9.30am–6.30pm, Sat, Sun to 7pm, rest of year daily 9.30am–5.30pm** ☎ 391 29 61 • Am Grossen Stern, Strasse des 17. Juni 🚌 100, 106, 187

Haus der Kulturen der Welt (D3) Known as "the pregnant oyster", or "Jimmy Carter's smile", the congress hall (1957) presents concerts, festivals and exhibitions from the world's five continents. Its reflecting pond has a bronze sculpture by Henry Moore. The 68 bells of the black granite Carillon tower in the Tiergarten opposite chime at noon and 6 pm. • **Daily except Mon 10am–9pm (variable according to exhibitions)** ☎ 39 78 70/39 78 71 75 • John-Forster-Dulles-Allee 10 Ⓢ Hauptbahnhof, Unter den Linden 🚌 100, M85

Reichstag, Deutscher Bundestag (E3) One of the great achievements of German democracy has been to overcome the sombre image of this massive 19th-century parliamentary building and make it downright popular. Two foreign artists have contributed to the transformation. In 1995, Bulgarian conceptual artist Christo wrapped the building up in fabric and attracted 5 million visitors. People were suddenly charmed by the place whose fire in 1933 had enabled Hitler to destroy freedom for 12 years. In 1999, British architect Norman Foster completed its magical glass dome, imparting a new lightness to the whole edifice. The dome is open to the public, accessible by elevator and spiral ramp to the very top. The inscription over the western portico, *Dem Deutschen Volke* (To the German People) suddenly makes more sense. Do not miss the Chancellery, completed in 2001. The office of the Chancellor is in a 9-storey cube. • **Dome open daily 8am–midnight (last entry 10 pm). For the rest of the building, visits by appointment. Roof-garden restaurant by reservation only** ☎ **22 62 99 33**

CHANGING STATIONS

In the years of divided Berlin, Bahnhof Zoo was the major railway station for trains arriving from western Germany and was notorious for the marginal outsiders squatting its halls all day long. Today, its bustling, late-closing shopping centre has transformed the station into a much brighter, more "user-friendly" place, two of its star attractions being the city's biggest international newspaper shop and the stand selling what connoisseurs consider to be Germany's best pretzels. The new glass and steel main station, Lehrter Bahnhof, has taken 10 years to build. Designed to receive a daily traffic of 2,400 passengers, it is within walking distance of the Chancery, Reichstag and other parliamentary buildings.

Open daily 9am–4.30pm; 6.30pm–midnight ☎ 227 32 152 • Platz der Republik Ⓢ Unter den Linden 🚌 100, M85, TXL

Bundeskanzleramt – Band des Bundes (D–E3)
Spread over a bend in the Spree is a row of buildings designed by Berlin architects Axel Schultes and Charlotte Frank for the new government district. The so-called "federal ribbon" starts in the west in the Kanzlerpark on the right bank of the river. The gleaming glass and white concrete 9-storey cube of the German Chancellor's new office and residence, the Bundeskanzleramt, stands in the northeast corner of the Tiergarten. A commanding presence, it opened in 2001 and looks across a broad esplanade (where more construction is planned) at the parliamentary office building, **Paul-Löbe-Haus**, linked by a footbridge to its twin, the **Marie-Elisabeth-Lüders-Haus**. Like the Reichstag's new dome, their architectural accent on glass transparency is a clear political statement for the newly unified German democracy. • Ⓢ **Unter den Linden**

Hamburger Bahnhof—Museum für Gegenwart (E2) On the north side of the Spree, the old railway station (1847) has been converted into a museum of contemporary art, showing works by Baselitz, Beuys, Kiefer, Lichtenstein, Rauschenberg, Twombly and Warhol, as well as special exhibitions. The controversial Flick Collection is displayed here in the Rieckhallen. • Tues–Fri 10am–6pm, Sat 11am–8pm, Sun 1am–6pm ☎ 39 78 34 11 • Invalidenstrasse 50/51 Ⓤ Zinnowitzer Strasse Ⓢ Hauptbahnhof 🚌 120, 123, 147, 240, 245, M85, TXL

◀ *Andy Warhol's iconic portrait of Mao (1973) in the Museum für Gegenwart.*

WALKING TOUR: TIERGARTEN

Turn left on Holstein Ufer along the **River Spree** and cross Moabiter bridge past a charming little children's playground to the U-shaped **Bundesministerium des Inneren** (Interior Ministry), westernmost of the government's new buildings. A bust of Konrad Zuse (1910–95) celebrates the "Father of the Computer", and another represents the novelist Thomas Mann (1875–1955). Back across the bridge at Bartningallee 29, stock up for your Tiergarten picnic at the venerable pastry shop **Konditorei Buchwald**, famous since 1852 for its *Baumkuchen* (tiered sponge cake). Then follow the river east to the 18th-century presidential palace, **Schloss Bellevue**, which shares a park with the president's oval office building, **Bundespräsidialamt** (1998). The old royal hunting park of the **Tiergarten** extends east of Spreeweg, alternating *Liegewiesen*, green spaces for lounging about, with *Grillwiesen* where barbecues are permitted. At Lutherbrücke, turn right on John-Foster-Dulles-Allee and look across the river at a serpentine apartment complex known as the **Bundesschlange** (Federal Snake) where parliamentarians were supposed to dwell in happy harmony (most live elsewhere). South of the river is the **Haus der Kulturen der Welt**, the "Pregnant Oyster" cultural centre (Berliners like quaint nicknames) and its 68-bell **Carillon** tower. Turn right on Paul-Löbe-Allee alongside the **Bundeskanzleramt** (2002), the German Chancellor's imposing offices. In front, along the north side of the esplanade, follow Otto-von-Bismarck-Allee past the stately 19th-century **Swiss Embassy** (Schweizer Botschaft) to Adenauer-Strasse and across Santiago Calatrava's elegant white **Kronprinzenbrücke**. It replaces the 18th-centuy Oberbaumbrücke toll-bridge. Turn right on Schiffbauerdamm to two sparkling new, deliberately transparent parliamentary office buildings, **Marie-Elisabeth-Lüders-Haus** and, linked by a footbridge, **Paul-Löbe-Haus**, named after distinguished parliamentarians of the pre-Hitler era. At the end of the bridge, go down the steps to the Spree and stroll towards the **Reichstag**, officially known as the Deutscher Bundestag. This building attracts a constant stream of tourists to visit the glass dome which British architect Norman Foster added, as he is said to have remarked, to "let German citizens peer down at their elected representatives".

TIERGARTEN 65

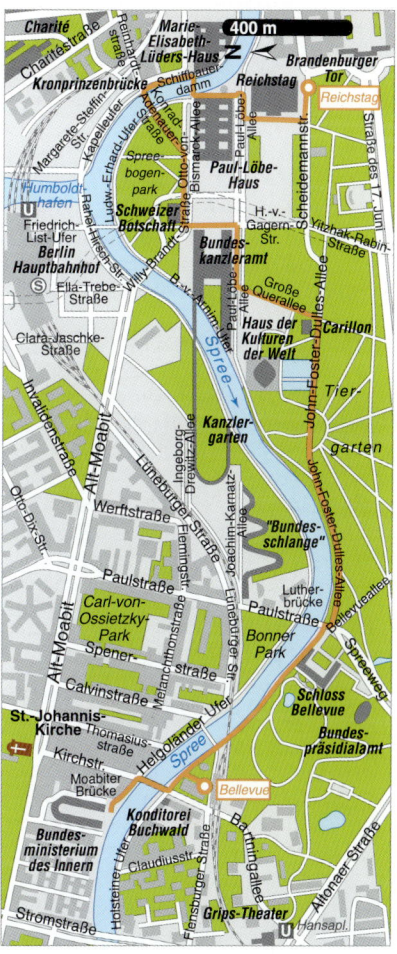

GOVERNMENT QUARTER IN THE TIERGARTEN

Take a river and park walk in the Tiergarten where the buildings of Germany's political leaders are observed by the city's joggers, strollers, lovers and picnickers.

Start:
Ⓢ Bellevue

Finish:
🚌 100 Reichstag

BERLIN FOR CHILDREN

There is plenty of fun for children in Berlin of all ages—sports galore, swimming and rollerblading in spring and summer, ice-skating and sledging in winter. There are ways to make even sightseeing enjoyable.

Touring the City

Boat cruises on the River Spree, the Landwehr Canal and the River Havel are a great—above all, *restful*—way to see the town. Many of the cruises can be boarded at the Museumsinsel, Schlossbrücke (Charlottenburg), Wannsee and Treptower Park. A pleasant alternative is the horse-drawn bus through the Niklolaiviertel. Bicycles can be rented with a rear seat added on for children.

Among the most popular monuments, mostly for their view, are the glass dome of the **Reichstag** and the 207-m-high revolving Telecafé restaurant on the **Fernsehturm**. One of the best ways to get children to accept a trip to the wonderful Egyptian collection in the **Neues Museum** so that you can see Nefertiti, is the promise that they will also get a look up close at some 3,000-year-old mummies (from autumn 2009). Combine your visit to **Schloss Charlottenburg** with a picnic in the castle gardens. A trip out to Dahlem and its museums of Asian art can include a visit to **Domäne Dahlem** (Königin-Luise Strasse 49, **U** Dahlem-Dorf) where a small museum has exhibits devoted to the old village farm life, with a little zoo for children to see and stroke the farm animals.

Playgrounds

Play areas with good, safe equipment are to be found in the Tiergarten, the Grunewald and other parks and squares all over town. One of the best neighbourhood playgrounds is the **Park am Wasserturm** in Prenzlauer Berg. At the nearby **Bauspielplatz** (Building Playground, Kollwitzstrasse 37), kids are encouraged to try their hand at craftwork in wood, stone and metal.

Sports

Rollerblading has become a favourite family sport and hundreds, sometimes thousands, take part in a communal **"skate by night"** parade through traffic-free streets every Sunday evening (when it doesn't rain) from May or June to the end of August. The start and finish is on Alexanderplatz and sets off in the direction of Karl-Marx-Allee at 8.30pm. The full 28-km (17-mile) tour follows varying circuits along the Landwehr Canal through Kreuzberg, Tiergarten and Charlottenburg. (Skates for hire at the Ski-Shop Charlottenburg, Schustehrusstrasse 1 ☎ 341 4870.)

Best swimming in summer—as well as other water sports and beach volleyball—is on the sandy beaches out at **Strandbad Wannsee**. In winter, the ice-skating is great when the smaller **Schlachtensee** freezes over—or on the ice rink at Potsdamer Plate.

For football fans, the **Olympiastadion** is the home ground of the city's Bundesliga club, Hertha Berlin. The stadium also stages international athletics championships.

Shopping

The ultimate in teddy bears and an amazing array of other cuddly, stuffed animals can be found at the **Steiff in Berlin** shop, Kurfürstendamm 220 ☎ 8862 5158. For the city's largest selection of every imaginable toy from dolls to the latest generation of electronic games, go straight to the 5th floor of the **KaDeWe** department store, Tauentzienstrasse 21 ☎ 212 10. As the name suggests, **Bonbonmacherei Kolbe & Stecher**, Oranienburger Strasse 32, Mitte ☎ 4405 5243, is a shop where you can watch them make their own sweets (except July and August when humidity in the air makes it technically impossible!)

CHARLOTTENBURG

Cutting through the centre of Charlottenburg is the Kurfürstendamm, literally the Prince Elector's Embankment, known as the Ku'damm. At its eastern end, where it turns into Tauentzienstrasse, it retains an imperial symbol with the Kaiser-Wilhelm-Gedächtniskirche. It extends westwards 3.5 km (2 miles) to the more humble Halensee railway station.

THE DISTRICT AT A GLANCE

SIGHTS

Architecture
U-Bahn-Wittenbergplatz 70
Schloss Charlottenburg ★ 73

Browsing
Europa-Center..........69
KaDeWe ★ 69
Kurfürstendamm ★ ..70
Savignyplatz ★ 71

History
The Story of Berlin ...73

Memorial
Kaiser-Wilhelm-Gedächtnis-Kirche ★ 68
Jüdisches Gemeindehaus 71

Museums
Museum für Fotografie – Helmut Newton Stiftung......70
Käthe Kollwitz-Museum 71

Museum Berggruen...............74
Bröhan Museum....74
Sammlung Scharf-Gerstenberg ★ 74

Sport
Olympiastadion 75

WALKING TOUR 76

WINING AND DINING 103

Kaiser-Wilhelm-Gedächtnis-Kirche (B4) The ruin of the Kaiser Wilhelm Memorial Church (1895) and its modern additions together form one of Berlin's most important symbols of World War II and peacetime recovery. With characteristic irreverence, Berliners puncture its poignancy by referring to its bomb-smashed spire as the "broken tooth", and the more recent hexagonal belltower and octagonal chapel with their walls of blue stained-glass as the "lipstick" and "powder compact". More serious visitors will appreciate in the memorial hall of the neo-Romanesque church the carved reliefs and friezes honouring the Hohenzollern rulers. • Mon–Sat 10am–6pm, several guided tours per day ☎ 218 50 23 • Breitscheidplatz Ⓤ Kurfürstendamm, Zoologischer Garten

CHARLOTTENBURG

The ruins of Kaiser-Wilhelm-Gedächtnis-Kirche have been preserved as a reminder of grimmer days.

Zoologischer Garten 🚌 Bus 100, 109, 110, 145, 200, 204, 245, M19, M29, M46, X9, X10, X34

Europa-Center (C5) Sharing Breitscheidplatz with the Kaiser Wilhelm Memorial Church, this high-rise shopping centre includes a hotel, cinemas and offices. It was a quite conscious proclamation of 1960s consumer capitalism in the Cold War contest with East Berlin. The Mercedes-Benz star was equally explicitly placed on top of its 22-storey tower as an emblem of Western luxury. Down below on the square, people gather around the amiable granite **Weltkugelbrunnen** (Fountain of Planet Earth) without giving too much thought to its symbolism. • Tauentzienstrasse 9–12 🚇 Wittenbergplatz, Zoologischer Garten Ⓢ Zoologischer Garten 🚌 Bus M19, M29, M46

KaDeWe (C5) Located not far from the Ku'damm along Tauentzienstrasse, this most opulent of department stores bears as its full name Kaufhaus des Westens (Department Store of the West), its totally unideological title since it was opened in 1907. Nonetheless, its most memorable day in recent years was November 10, 1989, the morning after the Wall came down. Even if most East Berliners could not afford its French and Italian designer clothes and the mind-boggling array of exotic delicacies in the food halls, this was the place where they wanted to see what they had been missing for all those years. Go up to the top floor restaurant (next to those splendid food halls with their beautiful dark wood shelves) and look at the Berlin rooftops through the semi-circular window, beneath the meccano-like girders holding up the roof. • Mon–Thurs 10am–8pm, Fri 10am–9pm, Sat 9.30am–8pm ☎ 21 21 0 • Tauentzienstrasse 21–24 **U** Wittenbergplatz 🚌 M19, M29, M46

U-Bahn Wittenbergplatz (C5) This is one U-Bahn station, the most handsome in Berlin, that is worth looking at as an urban monument. It was first built in 1902, to a design by Paul Wittig, as the centrepiece of the major commercial hub of what was already known as "City-West". It was expanded in 1912, and drastically modernized after World War II. Fortunately the exterior has now been restored to its former neoclassical glory, and the splendid fittings returned to the entrance hall.

Museum für Fotografie – Helmut Newton Stiftung (C5) Under one roof, the Photography Museum presenting temporary exhibitions and the Helmut Newton Foundation. The Australian photographer was born in Berlin in 1920 (originally Helmut Neustädter) and emigrated from Germany in 1938. • **Daily except Mon 10am–6pm, Thurs 10am–10pm** ☎ 31 86 48 25 • Jebensstrasse 2 **U** **S** Zoologischer Garten 🚌 100, 109, 110, 200, 204, 245, 249, M45, M46, M49, X9, X10, X34

Kurfürstendamm (A–B5) This bright and breezy avenue enjoyed two heydays in the 20th century. In the Golden Twenties, it was the hub of the city's elegant new theatre, restaurant and shopping area, the Neuer Westen (New West) competing with the established pomp of Unter den Linden and the more brassy flair of Friedrichstrasse. In the Cold War years, it was the showcase street of West Berlin and in 1989 the first place East Berliners made for when the Wall came down. Today, it has to compete with the revival of eastern Berlin, but its

CHARLOTTENBURG 71

essence of bourgeois chic is still there in the smart boutiques, theatres, cinemas and cafés. Like its rival, Unter den Linden, the Ku'damm had started as part of a bridle path, between the city centre and the royal hunting lodge in Grunewald forest. Bismarck came back after the Prussians' 1871 victory in Paris determined to turn it into a Champs-Elysées. Fashionable landmarks along the way include the **Kempinski Hotel**, where people who can't afford a room splash out on a drink at the grand Bristol Bar. At the west end of the avenue, the **Schaubühne** avant-garde theatre is part of Erich Mendelssohn's 1920s "Woga" complex, revolutionary for its time in combining in one building cinema, cabaret, shops, hotel and apartments.

Jüdisches Gemeindehaus (B5) North of the Ku'damm, set back on a courtyard, the Jewish Community Centre is a modern building that has incorporated as its entrance the domed portal of the synagogue destroyed by the Nazis on Kristallnacht (Crystal Night), November 9, 1938. The centre includes a synagogue and a small library open to the public. ☎ 88 02 80 • Fasanenstrasse 79–80 Ⓤ Uhlandstrasse, Kurfürstendamm, Zoologischer Garten Ⓢ Zoologischer Garten 🚌 109, 110, 245, 249, M19, M29, M45, M49, X10, X34

Käthe Kollwitz Museum (B5) Housed in an elegant villa, this small museum displays sculpture and sketches by Kollwitz (1867–1945). Born in Königsberg, she studied in Berlin and married a doctor who worked in a poor area of the city. Her home and studio in Prenzlauer Berg were destroyed by bombs in 1943. • Daily 1am–6pm ☎ 882 52 10 • Fasanenstrasse 24 Ⓤ Uhlandstrasse, Kurfürstendamm Ⓢ Zoologischer Garten 🚌 109, 110, 204, 249, M19, M29, X10

Savignyplatz (B5) Beyond the arches of the rather forbidding elevated railway, this tree-shaded square and its three offshoots—Carmer-, Knesebeck- and Grolmanstrasse—are frequented by numerous artists, writers, actors and their groupies. The area is full of bookshops, art galleries, gourmet restaurants and grungy-chic bars. The fauna here may remind you of the colourful characters satirized by Berlin painter George Grosz in the 1920s. Upon his return from exile in the United States in 1959, he made one last round of the bars before dying at Savignyplatz 6. Ⓢ Savignyplatz 🚌 M49, X34

CHARLOTTENBURG 73

The Story of Berlin (B5) A state-of-the-art multimedia display documenting the history of Berlin, from its foundation in 1237 to the present day. Guided tours are given in 12 languages. A time tunnel, a series of "event rooms" and 3-D sound systems take you back into the past. Particularly impressive is the anti-atomic bunker, built deep down beneath ground level, which gives you the weird feeling of reliving the Cold War. • Daily 10am–8pm, last admission 6pm ☎ 887 20 100 • Kurfürstendamm 207–208 **U** Uhlandstrasse, Kurfürstendamm **S** Savignyplatz 🚌 109, 110, M19, M29, X10

Schloss Charlottenburg (map 3 a2–3) Queen Sophie Charlotte's summer residence was begun on an intimate scale in 1695 and grew by the 18th century into one of Prussia's finest baroque edifices. Johann Friedrich Eosander designed the lofty dome and the west wing's Orangerie, while Georg von Knobelsdorff added the comely east wing for Friedrich the Great. Originally commissioned for the Berliner Schloss, Andreas Schlüter's bronze equestrian statue of Friedrich-Wilhelm (1697) ended up in the courtyard here in 1952. It had to be rescued from Tegel lake after it sank with a barge fleeing World War II bombardment. Interior furnishings destroyed in the war have been replaced by pieces taken from other baroque Prussian palaces. In the Royal Apartments, the major attractions are the **Porzellankabinett** of Japanese and Chinese porcelain from the 17th and 18th centuries, the richly decorated **Eosanderkapelle** (Eosander Chapel) and the **Eichengalerie** (Oak Gallery), the exquisite setting then and now for chamber music recitals.

◀ *Lush gardens surround the baroque Schloss Charlottenburg.*

The majority of the palace's magnificent art collection is housed on the first floor of the east wing, most notably the eight French masterpieces by Watteau in the **Goldene Galerie** ballroom, named for its gilded stucco. The palace gardens, one of the Berliners' favourite green spaces, combine formal French and "natural" English landscaping. The Italian-style **Schinkel-Pavillon** was added near the entrance to the east wing in 1824. Porcelain from the Königliche Porzellan-Manufaktur is displayed in the baroque **Belvedere** north of the carp pond.
• Old Castle (Altes Schloss) daily except Mon, Nov–Mar 10am–5pm; Apr–Oct 10am–6pm. New wing: daily except Tues, Apr–Oct 10am–6pm; Nov–Mar 10am–5pm ☎ 030 32 09 11 • Spandauer Damm 20–24 Ⓤ Richard-Wagner-Platz, Sophie-Charlotte-Platz Ⓢ Westend 🚌 109, 309, M45

Museum Berggruen (map 3 a3) In this museum, created in 1996 from the collection of Heinz Berggruen, the emphasis is on Picasso and his contemporaries. Over 100 paintings and sculptures trace the Spanish master's career, alongside works by Van Gogh, Cézanne, Braque, Klee, Matisse and Giacometti. Berggruen died in 2007; in order to show the latest acquisitions of his family, the museum will expand into a neighbouring building by 2011. • Daily except Mon 10am–6pm ☎ 32 69 58 15 • Schlossstrasse 1 Ⓤ Richard-Wagner-Platz, Sophie-Charlotte-Platz Ⓢ Westend 🚌 109, 309, M45

Bröhan Museum (map 3 a3) The Karl Bröhan collection—the gift of a merchant from Hamburg— presents all the artistic tendencies between 1889 and 1939: Jugendstil (Art Nouveau) and Art Deco furniture, silverware, porcelain, glassware and sculpture, with paintings by Max Liebermann and Lovis Corinth and others. • Daily except Mon 10am–6pm ☎ 32 69 06 00 • Schlossstrasse 1a Ⓤ Richard-Wagner-Platz, Sophie-Charlotte-Platz Ⓢ Westend ☎ 109, 309, M45

Sammlung Scharf-Gerstenberg (map 3 a3) Opened in July 2008, this museum presents a collection of artworks grouped under the title "Surreal Worlds" and dedicated to the Surrealists and their forerunners. Here you can ponder the meaning of painters such as Piranesi, Goya, Redon, Dalí, Magritte, Max Ernst and Dubuffet. The 250 works were gathered by Otto Gerstenberg

(1848–1935), whose collection was continued by his grandsons Walter and Dieter Scharf. • Daily except Mon 10am–6pm ☎ 34 35 73 12 • Schlossstrasse 70 Ⓤ Richard-Wagner Platz, Sophie-Charlotte-Platz Ⓢ Westend 🚌 109, 309, M45

Olympiastadion (off map by A4) Home of the Hertha Berlin football club, the oval stadium was originally built for the 1936 Summer Olympic Games and handsomely renovated for Germany's hosting the finals of the 2006 World Cup. An elegant glass and steel roof shelters the seating for 76,000 spectators. Apart from football, the stadium is also used for congresses and concerts. Only the Marathon Gates retain distant memories. • **Individual or guided tours available** ☎ 25 00 23 22 • Olympischer Platz Ⓤ Ⓢ Olympiastadion 🚌 104

CURRYWURST

One dark and stormy night in 1949, at a kiosk serving snacks at the corner of Kantstrasse and Kaiser-Friedrich-Strasse, Frau Herta Heuwer created what Berliners now insist on calling a delicacy, the *Currywurst*. This fat sausage, spiced with ketchup, chilli, Worcester sauce and a generous amount of Herta's newly discovered curry powder, guaranteed to offer splendid personal central heating on any cold day, became a national sensation, 800 million are now sold each year. Frau Heuwer (memorial plaque at Kantstrasse 101) registered her recipe at the German Patent Office in Munich, but variations have popped up everywhere ever since. Served with onions, chips and a roll to mop up the sauce, this satisfying snack is enjoyed by prominent bourgeois and proletarian gourmets alike. Three-star locations: *Curry 195*, Kurfürstendamm 195, big with the film festival crowd (serves champagne); *Curry 36*, Mehringdamm 36, for Kreuzberg artists and groupies; *Konnopke's Imbiss*, Schönhauser Allee 44a in Prenzlauer Berg.

WALKING TOUR: CHARLOTTENBURG

Cross the green and pleasant public garden on **Savignyplatz** to Grolmannstrasse at the northwest corner for a leisurely start at **Café Savigny** (No. 54) with a coffee and great choice of international newspapers. Its neighbour, the **Florian** restaurant bar, is a perennial favourite with the show biz crowd. From Savignyplatz, turn left on Kantstrasse to the ultramodern **Design Center** (1999, No. 17–20). Turn right on Uhlandstrasse and enter **Kempinski Plaza** (No. 181–183) for a look at the galleries and boutiques in its arcade and courtyard, a characteristic but updated feature of City West *Innenhof* architecture. Back on Uhlandstrasse, continue south to **Kurfürstendamm** and turn left to the grand **Kempinski Hotel**. Its café terrace on the corner of Fasanenstrasse has replaced the old Café Kranzler as *the* people-watching place on the Ku'damm.

Head north on Fasanenstrasse past the old headquarters of the **Bankhaus Löbbecke** (No. 76–77) housed in the elegant 19th-century Villa Ilse, now linked by a bridge to the bank's new office building. It stands next to the **Jüdisches Gemeindehaus** synagogue (an influx of some 11,000 Eastern European immigrants has made Berlin's Jewish community once again the biggest in Germany). Across the street beyond the S-Bahn tracks is the charming ivy-covered **Künstlerhaus St. Lukas**, a beautifully restored house built in 1890. Originally it was occupied by a score of sculptors, and even now some of its apartments and studios are used by artists. On the corner of Kanstrasse, preceded by a streetside waterfall, is the striking **Kant-Dreieck** office building (1995), crowned by a huge metal "sail" or "cock's comb", depending on your imagination. Across Kantstrasse, **Theater des Westens** is Charlottenburg's celebrated home of musical comedy, built in 1896 with an eclectic mix of medieval and Renaissance styles.

On the south side of Kantstrasse, cut through the modern shopping mall of Helmut Jahn's **Neues Kranzlereck** (2000) to the Ku'damm. Cross and turn right to head south on Fasanenstrasse for lunch or tea in the garden of the 19th-century **Literaturhaus** bookshop (No. 23–27).

CHARLOTTENBURG

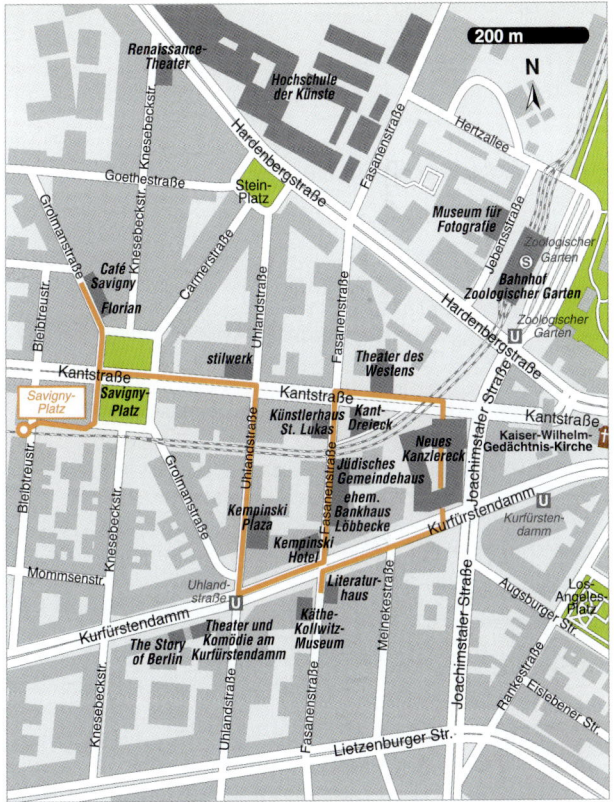

"CITY WEST", AROUND SAVIGNYPLATZ AND THE KU'DAMM

The cosmopolitan "City West" centres on Savignyplatz, attracting since the 1920s the artists and café society tucked away behind the showcase Kurfürstendamm.

Start: ⓢ Savignyplatz   **Finish:** Ⓤ Uhlandstrasse

RETAIL THERAPY

Appointed a UNESCO City of Design in 2006, Berlin is a magnet for European fashion; alongside countless luxury boutiques such as Gucci, Etro and Strenesse, shoppers will discover hundreds of original little shops illustrating the creativity of Berlin's young designers.

Department stores and shopping streets

The area around the Kurfürstendamm in Charlottenburg is very popular, and includes several side streets: Meineke-, Uhland-, Knesebeck-, Bleibtreu- and Fasanenstrasse. Art and antique dealers, fashion boutiques, luxury shops and arcaded shopping galleries often occupy the lower floors of handsome late-19th century buildings. On Tauentzienstrasse, you can't miss **KaDeWe**, the biggest and most famous of Berlin's department stores, with its magnificent food halls on the 6th floor—the bread! the cheeses! the teas and coffees! Everything is beautifully packaged and displayed. If you are looking for well-designed basic commodities or home furnishings, head straight for **stilwerk**, Kantstrasse 17, a smart mall incorporating 60 different stores. In Berlin-Mitte, Friedrichstrasse is a famed shopping street. The French architect Jean Nouvel designed the **Galeries Lafayette** on the corner of Französische Strasse, a branch of the famous Parisian department store, with a gourmet food department. To the south, forming an integral part of the Friedrichstadt Arcades, is the spectacular **Departmentstore im Quartier 206**, an extravagant creation by New York architect Henry Cobb, housing international trendy designer shops. The **Hackesche Höfe**, a series of courtyards, and the surrounding streets (Oranienburger Strasse, Auguststrasse, Rosenthaler Strasse) together form an interesting blend of art and commerce. Other great places for shopping are the **Galeria Kaufhof** and **ALEXA** on Alexanderplatz, and the modern malls on Potsdamer Platz.

Designer boutiques

Clothing, accessories and original, imaginative costume jewellery by more than 100 designers are sold at **Berlinomat** (Frankfurter Allee 89, Friedrichshain). At Neuer Schönhauser Strasse 10, the boutique **To Die For** has a more limited but equally irresistible array of jewellery, bags, belts and so on. The Berlin designer **Molotov** (Gneisenaustrasse 11, Kreuzberg) offers high-class, timeless fashions, while **Evelin Brandt** has several outlets around town selling elegant, classical women's wear (Savignyplatz 6, Charlottenburg; Friedrichstrasse 153A). The area around the Hackesche Höfe is a mecca for anyone with a shoe fetish: international makes are sold in ultra-chic shops such as **Orlando** (Oranienburger Strasse 7, Rosenthaler Strasse 48) and **Blutorange** (Neue Schönhauser Strasse 6–7). **MilkBerlin** (Torstrasse 102) sells hard-wearing waterproof bags from tarpaulin. For out-of-the-ordinary accessories and vintage ornaments for your home, head for **Schönhauser Design** (Neue Schönhauser Strasse 18).

Markets

The weekend is the time for mooching around the open-air flea markets. Clothing, jewellery, antiques and objets d'art can be found at the **Kunst- und Trödelmarkt Strasse des 17. Juni** (Sat and Sun 10am–5pm) and at the **Kunst- und Nostalgiemarkt am Zeughaus** near Museumsinsel (Sat and Sun 11am–5pm). But don't count on finding a bargain. For more reasonable prices, try the **Flohmarkt am Mauerpark** (Bernauer Strasse 63/64, Sun 9am–6pm), **Trödelmarkt am Arkonaplatz** (Sun 10am–5pm) or **Trödelmarkt Boxhagener Platz** (Friedrichshain, Sun 10am–6pm), frequented by non-professionals. During the week, you can browse around the **Antikmarkt Berlin**, held under the arches of the S-Bahn at Georgenstrasse 192–201 for paintings, furniture, lamps, jewellery and dolls (Wed–Mon 11am–6pm). Fruit and vegetable markets are held during the week, with stalls also selling cosmetics, clothing and jewellery. See, for example the **Winterfeldmarkt** at Schöneberg (Wed 8am–1pm, Sat 8am–4pm) or the Turkish community's **Türkische Markt** on Maybachufer in Kreuzberg (Tues and Fri noon–6.30pm).

PRENZLAUER BERG, FRIEDRICHSHAIN AND KREUZBERG

To see a more casual, cosmopolitan side of the city, explore eastern Berlin's old working-class and now artist-oriented district of Prenzlauer Berg, traditionally shortened to Prenzl'berg, northeast of Mitte. Its neighbour Friedrichshain draws lots of young people with its bars, cafés and clubs. Or venture into Kreuzberg, south of Mitte, another neighbourhood popular with artists and students but also home to the largest Turkish community outside Turkey.

THE DISTRICTS AT A GLANCE

SIGHTS

Architecture
Synagogue..............82

Atmosphere
Kollwitzplatz ★ 81
Jüdischer Friedhof....81
Kulturbrauerei 82
Friedrichshain..........83

Turkish Market ★ 84

Entertainment
Zeiss-Grossplanetarium....82

History
Gethsemanekirche...82

Museums
Jüdisches Museum ★ 84
Berlinische Galerie....84

Deutsches Technikmuseum 84
Schwules Museum...85

Landmark
Wasserturm.............82

WALKING TOUR 86

WINING AND DINING 106

PRENZLAUER BERG (G–H 1–2) This working-class district, created at the end of the 19th century with typical four- and five-storey apartment buildings and numerous back yards, was left to decline during the DDR years. In the 1980s it became the quarter for young artists and members of the opposition. Today there are very few of the decrepit old façades and even fewer are the artists who can afford to pay rents in the renovated buildings. What was just a few years an adventurous hive of creativity for adventurers is now an established nightlife district full of clubs, bars and pubs, and a number of young fashion designers have set up boutiques. The most popular areas are around

If you're looking for something arty, kitsch or vintage, browse around the streets of Prenzlauer Berg.

Kollwitz and Helmholtzplatz, Kastanienallee and Schönhauser Allee, Stargader Strasse and Zionskirchplatz.

Kollwitzplatz (H1) Named after 1920s sculptor Käthe Kollwitz and her doctor husband Karl, Kollwitzplatz has rapidly become a more easy-going but just as fashionable counterpart to western Berlin's Savignyplatz. Open-air café terraces and Italian, Greek, Alsatian and Russian restaurants lend the quarter a new cosmopolitan air. In the centre of the square is a bronze of Käthe Kollwitz, by Gustav Seitz after a self-portrait of the artist. To the north is Husemanstrasse, beautifully restored in the 1980s to its original stylish appearance. **U** Senefelderplatz **Tram** M2, M10

Jüdischer Friedhof (H1) Severely damaged in World War II, the Jewish Cemetery was restored in the 1990s. It is the last resting place of painter Max Liebermann, composer Giacomo Meyerbeer and publisher Leopold Ullstein. A lapidarium was created in 2005 to house the tombstones that could not be replaced in their original positions. • Mon–Thurs 8am–4pm, Fri 8am–1pm ☎ 441 98 24 • Schönhauser Allee 23–25 Ⓤ Senefelderplatz

Synagogue (H1) To serve its expanding congregation of Jewish immigrants from the former Soviet republics, Eastern Berlin's main synagogue has been beautifully refurbished in a rear courtyard. This one was preserved from fire in 1938 because adjacent apartments belonged to Nazi party officials. • **Guided tours only, Sun and Thurs** ☎ 88 02 83 16 • Rykestrasse 53 Ⓤ Senefelderplatz 🚋 M2

Wasserturm (H1) South of Kollwitzplatz is Wasserturm Park where a 19th-century British-built water tower, the first in Berlin, is the centre of a playground and terraced garden. At the foot of the tower, which is inhabited and sometimes used for cultural events, is a plaque that tells us that the engine house was used as a concentration camp in 1933. • Knaackstrasse 29 Ⓤ Senefelderplatz 🚋 M2

Kulturbrauerei (off map by H1) The Kulturbrauerei is a venerable red-brick brewery (1891) converted in 1991 into an arts complex for exhibitions and exhibitionist "happenings", cinema and theatre, featuring in particular Russian immigrant artists. There are several entrances. ☎ 44 31 51 51 • Schönhauser Allee 36–37, Knaackstrasse 97, Sredzkistrasse 1 Ⓤ Eberswalder Strasse 🚋 M1, M10, 12

Gethsemanekirche (off map by H1) The evangelical Gethsemane-Kirche (1891–1893) was a rallying point for "revolutionary" activity in 1989 that aimed to transform the GDR, and was consequently frequently the scene of open battles with the police. • Stargarder Strasse 77 Ⓤ Schönhauser Allee Ⓢ Schönhauser Allee 🚋 M1, 12

Zeiss–Grossplanetarium (off map by H1) Under the great shimmering silver dome of the planetarium, completed in 1987, is one of Europe's biggest and most modern observatories. • **Opening times vary according to events** • Prenzlauer Allee 80 ☎ 42 18 45 12 Ⓢ Prenzlauer Allee 🚋 M2 🚌 156

FRIEDRICHSHAIN (map 1 H–J 2–5) Beyond Prenzlauer Berg spreads the district of Friedrichshain. It is mostly frequented by students, young entrepreneurs and artists of various persuasions. The huge and popular **Volkspark Friedrichshain**, in the north part of the district, is the second-largest green space in the city, and includes paths, flower beds, lawns for sunbathing, and a large sports and leisure centre. Among the many sporting activities are beach volley and tennis courts, a skateboarding area, a climbing rock, and a toboggan run for winter, on one of the two hills built over anti-aircraft towers with rubble from World War II (and known as the Kleiner Bunkerberg). The main thoroughfare of Friedrichshain is the wide **Karl-Marx-Alléee**, built in the 1950s in Soviet style and lined with massive "Arbeiterpalasten", literally, palaces for workers, in a heavy Soviet style mixed with Schinkel-type classicism. **Simon-Dach-Strasse**, with its countless bistrots and boutiques, has become the main social gathering place of the district. For nightlife you can also wander over to Krossener Strasse, Boxhagener Strasse and Boxhagenerplatz, the Oberbaum bridge and Warschauer Strasse subway station. The **Oberbaum bridge**, at the end of Mühlenstrasse (along which stretches the East Side Gallery, the longest section of the Berlin Wall still standing) is the symbol of the district. It is a picturesque neo-Gothic construction with two towers and crenellated ramparts, and links Friedrichshain to Kreuzberg.

KREUZBERG (E–H 4–6, map 1 H–J 4–6) The neighbourhood takes its name from the hill in **Viktoria Park** (Ⓤ Platz der Luftbrücke) topped by Karl Friedrich Schinkel's neo-Gothic Nationaldenkmal (National Monument) and waterfall to commemorate Germany's defeat of Napoleon. There's an adventure park here, and a beergarden and restaurant with dance floor. **Bergmannstrasse**, leading east from there, is the main thoroughfare of the bourgeois southern part of Kreuzberg. In the 1970s and 80s, the neglected tenement buildings of the part of Kreuzberg north of the Landwehr canal, bordered by the Wall, were taken over by western Berlin's largest communities of squatters, punks and Turks. The area is still full of cafés, bars and clubs, and remains the centre of gay Berlin, but it has sobered up quite a lot since the Wall came down. **Oranienstrasse** (Ⓤ Moritzplatz) is the centre of Kreuzberg's Turkish community, which gathers around Kotbusser Tor, while the "alternative" communities of artists, media people and students mainly stick to the Schlesisches Tor area. Junk shops, health food stores and "New-Age" markets are sprouting up all over the district, together with Turkish shops and restaurants.

Turkish Market (map 1 H6) The noisy, crowded market spreading along the south bank displays all the spices, fruit, fish, exotic fabrics, carpets and household goods typical of any bazaar in Istanbul or Anatolia. Along the north bank of the canal, Paul-Lincke-Ufer, fashionable cafés and boutiques beneath elegant balconied apartments have been installed in Jugendstil (Art Nouveau) buildings, restored as part of the district's post-Wall gentrification. • **Tues, Fri noon–6.30pm** • Maybachufer **U** Kottbusser Tor

Jüdisches Museum (F5) Daniel Libeskind's astonishing design (1999) makes the Jewish Museum an experience in itself. Incorporating a handsome baroque Prussian courthouse of 1735, an elongated zigzagging concrete building suggests a dislocated Star of David. The narrow windows slash the grey walls like knife cuts. The old courthouse is the setting for the library and a Jewish restaurant but is also used for temporary exhibitions, films, concerts and lectures. The museum's permanent displays trace the rich and proud Berlin Jewish story, complemented architecturally by a bleak hollow tower symbolizing the climactic fact of the Holocaust. • **Daily 10am–8pm (Monday to 10pm)** ☎ 25 99 33 00 • Lindenstrasse 9–14 **U** Hallesches Tor 🚌 248, M29, M41

Berlinische Galerie (G5) The young and stylish municipal museum presents Berlin art, photography and architecture from 1879 to modern times. Temporary exhibitions put the accent on the avant-garde. • **Daily (except Tues) 10am–6pm** ☎ 78 90 26 00 • Alte Jakobstrasse 124–128 **U** Hallesches Tor, Kochstrasse, Spittelmarkt 🚌 M29, M41, 248

Deutsches Technikmuseum Berlin (E6) In this museum of technology, one of the biggest and far-reaching in the world, you will learn more than you ever wanted to know about vintage cars, steam engines, ships and planes, but also themes such as energy, light, printing, jewellery-making and aeronautics. Hands-on experiments in the Science Center Spectrum. • **Tues–Fri 9am–5.30pm, Sat, Sun 10am–6pm** ☎ 90 25 40 • Trebbiner Strasse 9 **U** Möckernbrücke, Gleisdreieck **S** Anhalter Bahnhof

Schwules Museum (off map by F6) The Gay Museum is a private institution dedicated to preserving and discovering homosexual history, art and culture, and documenting 200 years of homosexuality in Germany. The museum also has a library and archives. • **Daily except Tues 2–6pm, Sat to 7pm** ☎ 69 59 90 50 • Mehringdamm 61 🆄 Mehringdamm ☎ 140, 248

AMPELMANN: SUCCESS STORY IN RED AND GREEN

The Ampelmann, East Germany's very own quaint little mannikin to tell pedestrians at the traffic lights when to go and when to wait, has become a huge commercial success. You can see him on T-shirts, lamps, vases, umbrellas, bottle-openers, sweets and biscuits. At the country's 1990 reunification, the Ampelmann had landed with so many other symbols of the failed GDR, literally, on the rubbish dump, to be replaced by the more streamlined, less jolly Western icon. Fed up with losing all traces of their old identity, East Berliners fought to save him, teaming up with West German entrepreneur Marcus Heckhausen, who saw the icon's commercial potential as a logo, and its East German designer, Karl Peglau (who created it back in 1961). The first Ampelmann lamps went on sale in 1996 and a first shop opened in 2001 in the Hackesche Höfe. There are now four shops in Berlin and an Ampelmann Restaurant. Perhaps more importantly, in 2005, the city adopted the Ampelmann for traffic lights in western Berlin.

WALKING TOUR: PRENZLAUER BERG

Commemorating the early Socialist heroine assassinated in 1919, **Rosa-Luxemburg-Platz** is dominated by the venerable **Volksbühne** theatre which has staged both avant-garde and popular drama for nearly 100 years. The pavement of the square itself is engraved with 60 quotations of Rosa Luxemburg. On the south side is the equally historic **Kino Babylon**, Berlin's last remaining cinema from the era of silent film. Over to the northeast, the neighbourhood's Marxist tradition is upheld by the **Karl-Liebknecht-Haus**, HQ of the left-wing party Die Linke since 2007. Prenzlauer Berg's main thoroughfare Schönhauser Allee runs north to the triangular **Senefelderplatz**, honouring the inventor of lithography with a statue on which a cherub inscribes his name backwards, as it would appear on the lithographer's slab. Continue on Schönhauser Allee past the 19th-century **Jüdischer Friedhof** (Jewish Cemetery, Nos. 23–25) and turn right on Wörther Strasse to **Kollwitzplatz**, with Russian, Greek and Italian bars and restaurants surrounding Gustav Seitz's seated statue of the sculptress Käthe Kollwitz who lived in the neighbourhood with her doctor husband.

From the southern end of the square, take Kollwitzstrasse to the children's open-air playground **Kolle 37** where budding craftsmen learn to work with wood, clay, metal and felt. Turn left on Belforter Strasse and left again on Kolmarer Strasse to the **Wasserturm Park**—many streets here (Belfort, Strasbourg, Metz and Colmar) are named after conquests in the 1870 Franco-Prussian War. Now used for concerts and theatre shows, the water tower was built by the English Waterworks Company from 1852 to 1877 to provide Germany with its first running-water system. From Knaackstrasse north of the park, turn right on Rykestrasse past the neo-Romanesque **Synagogue** (1904) sheltered in a courtyard at No. 53. Turn left on Wörtherstrasse across the top of Kollwitzplatz and turn right on Knaackstrasse to the **Kulturbrauerei** at No. 75, the multicultural complex sprawling across the old Schultheiss brewery—with a couple of cafés serving beer for old time's sake. (Exit on Schönhauser Allee.)

PRENZLAUER BERG, FRIEDRICHSHAIN AND KREUZBERG 87

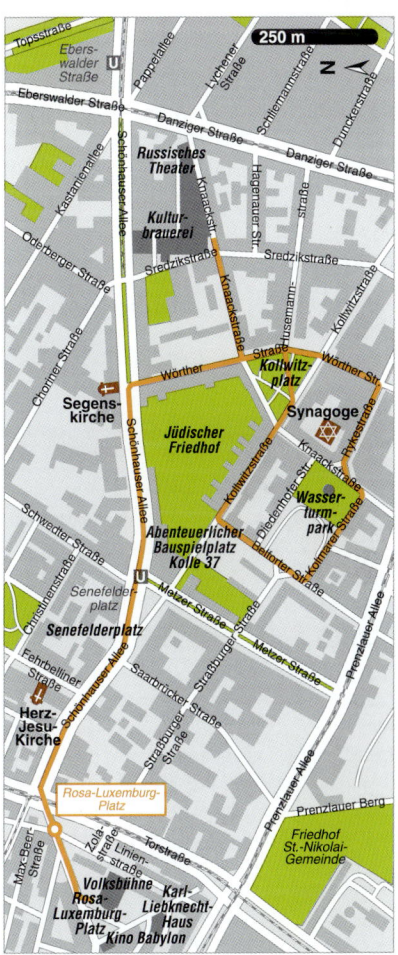

PRENZLAUER BERG
Eastern Berlin's old working-class "Prenzl'berg" takes on a new lease of life with the artists and students drawn to its cafés, bars and galleries.

Start:
U Rosa-Luxemburg-Platz

Finish:
U Eberswalder Strasse

EXCURSIONS

For rest and recreation, Berliners have no lack of greenery, with lakes, beaches and shady woodland within easy reach by train or bus. There is an interesting group of museums at Dahlem, and the city of Potsdam, capital of Brandenburg, is well worth a day trip to see its castle, Schloss Sanssouci.

THE DISTRICT AT A GLANCE

SIGHTS

Architecture
Potsdam Old Town ..92
Kolonie Alexandrowka.........93
Schloss Cecilienhof..95

Atmosphere
Köpenick.................88
Spandau 89
Dahlem.................90

Potsdam Dutch Quarter....................93

Entertainment
Filmpark Babelsberg...............95

Greenery
Botanischer Garten..90
Grunewald and Wannsee★ 91
Pfaueninsel 91

Landmarks
Zitadelle Spandau....90
Schloss Sanssouci★.93

Memorial
Haus der Wannsee-konferenz★ 91

Museums
Dahlem Museums★ 90
Brücke Museum★ ...91

WALKING TOUR 96

KÖPENICK (map 4 P3) Southeast of Berlin, the historic centre of the borough of Köpenick is built on an island at the confluence of the Spree river and the Dahme tributary. The most handsome dwellings of the old town (18th century) are on the Alter Markt and Alt-Köpenick street. The splendid red-brick neo-Gothic town hall (built 1901–03) boasts an imposing courtyard and monumental staircase. Outside stands a statue of the Captain of Köpenick, the impostor Wilhelm Voigt who in 1906 masqueraded as a Prussian military officer, commandeered six soldiers and occupied the city hall. On the Schlossinsel south of the Old Town is Schloss Köpenick, a 17th-century castle, restored at great expense between 1994 and 2004. It now houses a **Museum of Decorative Arts**

EXCURSIONS 89

When the Wannsee freezes over, Berliners take to their skates—at their own risk.

(closed Monday) devoted to home decoration and art of the Renaissance, baroque and rococo periods. East of the Old Town, Köpenick's lake, **Grosser Müggelsee**, is popular with Berliners for sailing and fishing. 🇸 Köpenick

SPANDAU (map 4 N2) West of Berlin, this ancient borough, older than Berlin itself, remains a country village a world apart from the metropolis. It obtained city rights in 1232 and was incorporated into Greater Berlin in 1920. At Breite Strasse 32, the oldest house has a 15th-century Gothic vaulted interior. On Markstrasse and Ritterstrasse are other noteworthy houses, with fine 17th- and 18th-century gables and arches. The late-Gothic Nikolaikirche on Reformationsplatz in the middle of the Old Town dates back to the 15th century, but the belfry is largely baroque and its altar 16th-century Renaissance. Prince Elector Joachim II is honoured with a bronze statue outside the main portal of the church for having bowed to the citizens' pressure to adopt their Protestant faith in 1539. 🇺 Altstadt Spandau, Rathaus Spandau 🇸 Spandau

Zitadelle Spandau In the northwest of town, the symbol of Spandau is its 16th-century red-brick Citadel, standing on the opposite bank of the Havel. It is one of the most important Renaissance fortresses of Europe. Four sharp bastions form the corners of this square citadel, which also encompasses a place (residence) and the older medieval Juliusturm (Julius Tower). A historic museum is set in the old arsenal. • Daily except Mon 10am–5pm ☎ 354 94 40 • Am Juliusturm Ⓤ Zitadelle 🚌 X33

DAHLEM (map 4 N3) The district of Dahlem, southwest of Berlin, near the forest of Grunewald and the Grosser Wannsee, is one of the most desirable and pleasant residential areas of the city. This old farming village is today home to the Free University, several renowned museums and a superb botanical garden. In the historic centre, you can visit the **Domäne Dahlem** open-air museum, an organic farm and petting zoo, and a museum of agriculture and nutrition. The Metro station of Dahlem-Dorf is also worth seeing; it's a picturesque half-timbered building with thatched roof, dating from 1913. Ⓤ Dahlem-Dorf

Botanischer Garten Berlin's "Green Jewel" and Europe's largest botanical garden covers an area of more than 43 ha and counts some 22,000 plant species. Apart from the fascinating greenhouses, you can stroll through various gardens, one specially devoted to fragrance and touch, another to mossses, one to medicinal plants, and a splendid arboretum, and marvel at the wonders of the plant world. • Daily May–July 9am–9pm, April, Aug 9am–8pm, Sept 9am–7pm, Mar, Oct 9am–6pm, Feb 9am–5pm, Nov–Jan 9am–4pm ☎ 83 85 01 00 • Königin-Luise-Platz, Unter den Eichen 5–10 Ⓤ Rathaus Steglitz, Dahlem-Dorf Ⓢ Botanischer Garten

Dahlem Museums During the years of the city's division, this group of museums southwest of the centre was the main focus of West Berlin's art collections. They have undergone extensive restructuring. The **Ethnologische Museum**, devoted to early art and artefacts of the Americas, Africa, Asia, the Pacific islands and non-German-speaking Europe, was the first to reopen. Then, in 2000, followed the **Museum für Asiatische Kunst** covering art from India and East Asia. The **Museum Europäischer Kulturen** (entrance at Arnimallee 25) presents European art and traditions from the 18th century to the present (closed for renovation from July 2009 to autumn 2010). • Tues–Fri 10am–6pm, Sat, Sun 11am–6pm ☎ 830 14 38 • Lansstrasse 8 **U** Dahlem-Dorf

Brücke-Museum This fine little museum, which opened in 1967, draws on a comprehensive collection of early 20th-century German Expressionist painters working in Dresden then in Berlin under the name Die Brücke (The Bridge, as a symbol of their group solidarity): Kirchner, Nolde, Heckel, Pechstein, Mueller and Schmidt-Rottluff. • Daily except Tues 11am–5pm ☎ 831 20 29 • Bussardsteig 9 **S** Zehlendorf 🚌 115, X10 Clayallee/Pücklerstrasse

GRUNEWALD AND WANNSEE (map 4 N2–M3) The forests and lakes of Grunewald southwest of the city have always provided Berliners with their most convenient recreation area. Never was this more vital than when West Berlin was cut off from the outside world by the Wall. Vast stretches of pine trees have been supplemented by handsome groves of chestnut, oak, birch, beech and lime, providing a protected habitat for wild boar, deer, foxes and hares. You get a great view over the region from the **Teufelsberg** at the northern edge of the Grunewald. It is the highest "mountain" of Berlin, 115 m high, created on a rubbish heap after World War II. A **hunting lodge** on the southeast shore of the Grunewaldsee, built in Renaissance style in 1542, is famous for its collection of works by Lucas Cranach the Elder and his son Hans. The shores of Wannsee, Krumme Lanke and Schlachtensee welcome bathers to sandy beaches complete with old-fashioned sheltered basket-seats. **S** Grunewald

Haus der Wannseekonferenz The Wannsee Conference House is an elegant bourgeois villa in pleasant surroundings where top Nazis made formal plans to execute Hitler's order for the extermination of Europe's Jews. Now converted into a museum, its documents, photographs and film relate the 1942 Wannsee conference, chaired by SS leader Reinhard Heydrich, and the results as organized by Adolf Eichmann, also present. • Daily 10am–6pm (closed on holidays) ☎ 805 00 10 • Am Grossen Wannsee 56–58, Zehlendorf **S** Wannsee, then 🚌 114

Pfaueninsel (map 4 M3) Take a short ferryride over the Havel River to Peacock Island, a nature reserve with soaring lodgepole pines, venerable oaks and a bird sanctuary. Among the English landscaped gardens are a romantic (but fake) castle ruin and Schinkel's charming Schweizer Haus (Swiss Cottage). Ⓢ Wannsee, then 🚍 218 and ferry

POTSDAM (map 4 M4) The capital of Brandenburg lies at the southwest corner of Berlin. In a delightful setting of royal palaces surrounded by parks and lakes, it displays a largely graceful facet of Prussia's history. The garrison town that the Sergeant King Friedrich-Wilhelm I created in the 18th century was transformed by his more sophisticated son, Friedrich the Great, into a haven for the arts and refinements of a more courtly life. The city's dominant feature today is still Sanssouci Palace, which he lovingly turned into a German Versailles. Under the Nazis, the town returned to its militaristic beginnings, with Hitler receiving the "blessing" of Field Marshal Hindenburg at the Garnisonkirche (destroyed after the war). Hitler's conquerors closed this chapter by meeting in Potsdam to divide up defeated Germany. In 1991, the coffins of the two kings were brought back to be buried at Sanssouci—Friedrich the Great on the palace terrace and his father some distance away in the Friedenskirche.
• 40 minutes by road or rail from the city centre Ⓢ Potsdam Hauptbahnhof

Old Town Potsdam's Altstadt area is still recovering from bombardments of 1945 and the later dismantling of Hohenzollern monuments by the East German communist government. On Alter Markt, Karl Friedrich Schinkel's neoclassical Nikolaikirche with its gigantic dome has been restored; it dominates the charming but more modest silhouette of the rebuilt 18th-century Altes Rathaus (Old Town Hall). The Knobelsdorff-

Potsdam's ▷ charming Dutch Quarter.

Haus (1750), nearby, is named after its architect. Of the Hohenzollerns' Stadtschloss (Town Palace) only the 17th-century Marstall remains, royal stables now converted to house the Film Museum. Construction of the new Brandenburg parliament building, which preserves the historic façade of the old castle, is due for completion in 2011. The main feature of old Potsdam is its shopping street, Brandenburger Strasse, lined with several 18th-century houses. It leads to the triumphal arch of the Brandenburg Gate (1770), preceding its famous Berlin counterpart by 21 years.

Dutch Quarter On and around Mittelstrasse, the Holländisches Viertel is one of the few aesthetic initiatives of the Sergeant King Friedrich-Wilhelm I. These handsome red-brick houses were built from 1734 to 1740 as homes for Dutch craftsmen. Most of them left and were replaced by an artists' colony, but their 130-odd houses form one of the region's most pleasant neighbourhoods. Many of the houses conceal delightful garden-taverns in their inner courtyards. The market on Bassinplatz offers an impressive array of local produce. Brandenburg vegetables and fruit are among the best in Germany, particularly the asparagus, apples, cherries and strawberries.

Kolonie Alexandrowka Potsdam's other "foreign" quarter is this self-contained Russian village created on the north side of town by Friedrich-Wilhelm III for veterans of the Napoleonic Wars, in honour of Tsar Alexander I. Descendants still live in the typical timbered datchas and worship at the onion-domed Russian Orthodox Alexander Nevski Chapel.

Schloss Sanssouci Friedrich the Great built himself a palace where he could pursue his tastes for music, art and philosophy without a worry—*sans souci*—about the affairs of state. Architect Georg von Knobelsdorff drew on the king's own sketches to create in 1745 an exquisite rococo residence forming a harmonious whole with its terraced vine-covered gardens. In the lovely Konzertzimmer, a 19th-century painting by Adolf von Menzel shows how Friedrich played flute there to the harpsichord of Carl Philip Emmanuel Bach, son of Johann Sebastian. The king kept his personal library of over 2,000 French books in the cedarwood Bibliothek of the east wing rotunda. French was also the language of his "philosophical suppers", held in the central Marmorsaal (Marble

Hall) and animated by Voltaire from 1750 to 1753. The palace gardens, in formal French design and landscaped English style, cover some 300 ha. Friedrich's **Bildergalerie** (Picture Gallery) east of the palace includes Flemish and Italian works by Van Dyck, Rubens, Caravaggio and Guido Reni. You can visit the gallery without a guide. Southwest of the terraced gardens, the **Chinesisches Haus** boasts gilded palm trees and a gilded mandarin on its pagoda roof. The immense **Neue Palais**, at the western end of the main avenue, was built by Frederick II after the Seven Years' War, as a symbol of Prussian might. • **Guided tours only, daily except Mon, Nov–Mar 10am–5pm, Apr–Oct 10am–6pm** ☎ (0331) 969 42 02 • Maulbeerallee 🚌 695, X15

Schloss Cecilienhof Joseph Stalin, Harry Truman and Winston Churchill met in this 19th-century English-style country manor to negotiate the Potsdam Treaty that carved up Germany in 1945. The ivy-covered residence is now a museum and hotel. • Daily except Mon, Apr–Oct 10am–6pm; Nov–Mar 10am–5pm ☎ (0331) 96 94 244 • Im Neuen Garten 🚋 92, 96 🚌 692

Filmpark Babelsberg (map 4 M3) Ideal for a day trip, this theme park includes stunt shows, 4D action cinema and many other attractions based on cinema and TV programmes. There are also guided tours of the old UFA Studios of Germany's cinema era of the 1920s and 30s. • Apr–Oct daily 10am–6pm; often closed Mon: check by phone ☎ (0331) 721 27 50 • Grossbeerenstrasse Ⓢ Babelsberg, then 🚌 690

◀ *Atlantes and caryatids representing the companions of Bacchus adorn the garden façade of Schloss Sanssouci.*

WALKING TOUR: POTSDAM

Named after the queen of Prussia who mothered 10 children, including the future Kaiser Wilhelm I, **Luisenplatz** has replaced its Communist-era car park with a small fountain and young lime trees. **Brandenburger Tor**—yes, Potsdam has one, too, a gate (1770) 21 years older than Berlin's and more ornate than monumental, still bears a sign *Schritt!* (Walking pace!) warning horse-riders not to gallop.

Preceded by a mosaic of the city's emblematic Prussian eagle in its paving, pedestrian-zoned **Brandenburger Strasse** is the town's main shopping street. Turn left on Hermann-Elflein-Strasse to the half-timbered façade of the house **Im Güldenen Arm**, the 18th-century home of a wealthy woodcarver and brewer (now an exhibition space). Double back and turn right on Gutenbergstrasse to the tree-lined **Lindenstrasse**, boasting some of the town's smarter boutiques and cafés. **Kaffeerösterei Junick** is favoured for its freshly roasted coffee and excellent apple strudel. Head north to the **Jägertor**, oldest of Potsdam's city gates topped by a stag fighting off hunting hounds. Beyond Hegelallee, turn right on Dortusstrasse and continue east on **Gutenbergstrasse**, to see its gabled half-timbered houses with an occasional glimpse of characteristic interior courtyards. A left turn on the busy Friedrich-Ebertstrasse leads to **Nauener Tor**, Germany's earliest example (1755) of neo-Gothic design, inspired by Friedrich the Great's liking for Scottish Highland castles.

Retrace your steps to turn left on Mittelstrasse into the heart of the **Holländisches Viertel**, now a colourful colony for artists and craftsmen. One of the best examples of the 128 Dutch red-brick homes remaining from the 18th century is the **Jan-Bouman-Haus** at Mittelstrasse 8, with an exhibit tracing the history of the neighbourhood. Walk south on Benkertstrasse over to Bassinplatz and the Catholic **Kirche St. Peter und Paul**, built in 1870 with a 64-m-high bell tower modelled on the campanile of St Zeno in Verona.

EXCURSIONS 97

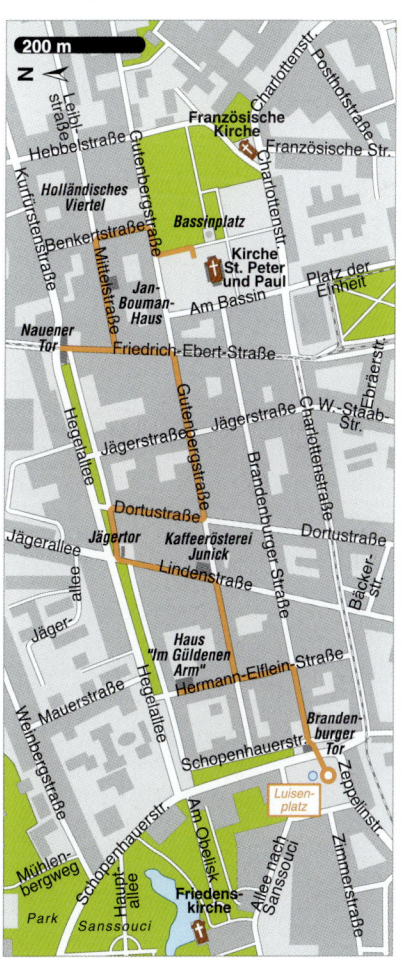

AROUND TOWN
Potsdam is not just a palace, it's a thriving town with an old-world atmosphere much more relaxed than the nearby metropolis over which its princes once ruled.

Start:
🚌 695 from Potsdam Hauptbahnhof to Luisenplatz

Finish:
🚋 90, 92 Friedrich-Ebertstrasse

cityBites

Berlin has restaurants for every taste and for every wallet, and you can eat your way around the world. The German answer to nouvelle cuisine is *neue deutsche Küche*, traditional German dishes prepared in a lighter, more imaginative manner. Our selection of restaurants follows the same order as the sightseeing chapters in this guide (pages 22–87), and an indication of prices for a typical meal is given by signs:

- 1 = under 17 euros
- 2 = 17–32 euros
- 3 = 32–55 euros
- 4 = over 55 euros

UNTER DEN LINDEN

Aigner
🚇 Französische Strasse
Französische Strasse 25
Mitte
☎ 203 75 18 50
Daily noon–2am, kitchen closes at 11.30pm
[2]

Regional cuisine with an Austrian accent; the classics are duck Brandenburger style, and *Tafelspitz*, boiled beef.

Borchardt
🚇 Französische Strasse
Französische Strasse 47
☎ 81 88 62 62
Daily 11.30am–1am
[3]

Elegant restaurant. Its grand dining room with marble columns is a meeting place for Berlin's political and cultural celebrities. French and Italian dishes.

Cafe Einstein
Ⓢ Unter den Linden
Unter den Linden 42
☎ 204 36 32
Daily 7am–10pm
[1]

Austrian café. In summer, the garden is the place to be seen.

Der Kartoffelkeller
🚇 Ⓢ Friedrichstrasse
Albrechtstrasse 14b
☎ 282 85 48
Daily 11am–1am
Reservation recommended
[1]

The potato is king in this restaurant where the humble tuber is transformed into all kinds of gourmet dishes, many from old cookbooks.

Die Eins
Ⓢ Unter den Linden
Wilhelmstrasse 67a
☎ 22 48 98 88
Mon–Sat 9am–1am,
Sun 10am–1am
[2]

Bar/restaurant on the banks of the Spree, not far from the Brandenburg Gate in the heart of the new government district. The summer terrace looks onto the Reichstag. October to May Sunday brunch with live music.

Dressler
Ⓢ Unter den Linden
Unter den Linden 39
☎ 204 44 22
Daily 8am–1am
[2]

Art Deco setting, reminiscent of the 1920s and 30s. French cuisine.

Fridas Schwester
Ⓢ Hackescher Markt
Neue Schönhauser Str. 11
☎ 28 38 47 10
Mon–Fri from 11am,
Sat, Sun from 10am
[2]

A colourful, inventive mix of international specialities; a fusion of cultures, cuisines and drinks. Sunday brunch 10am–5pm.

Las Cucarachas
Ⓢ Oranienburger Strasse
Oranienburger Strasse 38
☎ 282 20 44
Daily noon–2am
[1]

Cosy Mexican restaurant and bar with summer terrace. American and Tex-Mex food.

Operncafé
🚇 Ⓢ Friedrichstrasse
Unter den Linden 5
☎ 20 26 83
Café daily 8am–midnight
Restaurant daily noon–midnight
[2]

Berlin's biggest coffee house, with more than 50 different cakes and gateaux on the menu. It was built in 1733 and was the residence of the three daughters of Queen Louise of Hohenzollern, hence known as the Prinzessinnenpalais. View over the opera house.

Quarré im Adlon
Ⓢ Unter den Linden
Unter den Linden 77
☎ 22 61 15 55
Daily 6.30am–11pm
[4]

Quarré im Adlon

Berlin's most exclusive restaurant in the Hotel Adlon, with a view of the Brandenburg Gate. High-class French and German cuisine.

Ständige Vertretung (StäV)
U S Friedrichstrasse
Schiffbauerdamm 8
☎ 282 39 65
Daily 11am–1am
1
Cologne and its famous Kölsch-Bier brought to Berlin. Good food, noisy atmosphere; walls covered with newspaper cuttings and old photos of politicians.

Tadschikische Teestube
U Französische Strasse
Am Festungsgraben 1
☎ 204 11 12

Mon–Fri 5pm–midnight, Sat, Sun 3pm–midnight
1
Lay back against the cushions and enjoy a Tadjik tea ceremony and Russian snacks, all in an authentic atmosphere.

Yosoy
S Hackescher Markt
Rosenthaler Strasse 37
☎ 28 39 12 13
Daily from 11am
1
Enormous choice of *tapas* and Rioja served from the barrel. The seafood platter for two is well worth investigating.

ALEXANDERPLATZ

Ming Dynastie
U S Jannowitzbrücke
Brückenstrasse 6
☎ 30 87 56 80

Daily noon–midnight
1
Delicious, authentic Chinese specialities. Classical Chinese music accompanies your meal on Friday and Saturday evenings, as well as during the all-you-can-eat Sunday buffet.

Mutter Hoppe
U S Alexanderplatz
Rathausstrasse 21
☎ 241 56 25
Daily from 11.30am
1
Meat is high on the list of priorities of this restaurant proposing good German cuisine and live music Friday and Saturday.

Reinhard's im Nikolaiviertel
U S Alexanderplatz
Poststrasse 28

Ming Dynastie

☎ 242 52 95
Daily 9am–midnight
[2]

In the heart of the historic Nikolai district, a restaurant with a 1920s atmosphere, serving seasonal German cuisine.

Restauration Tucholsky
U Rosenthaler Platz
Torstrasse 189
☎ 281 73 49
Daily noon–midnight
[1]

Cosy German restaurant and plenty of documentation on the journalist and satirist Kurt Tucholsky (1890–1935).

Telecafé im Fernsehturm
U S Alexanderplatz
Tram Alexanderplatz
Panoramastrasse 1a
☎ 242 33 33
Daily 9am–midnight
[1]

German and international cuisine to set your head spinning. The café turns a full circle in 30 minutes, providing a sensational panorama over the city.

Unsicht-Bar
U Rosa Luxemburg-Platz
Gormannstrasse 14
☎ 24 34 25 00
Wed–Sun from 6pm
Reservation recommended
[3]

A different experience that will heighten your senses of smell, taste, touch and hearing. *Unsichtbar* means invisible, and in this restaurant the waiters and staff are blind or visually impaired. Once through the foyer you are literally and completely in the dark—no trace of light (such as cigarettes or mobile phone screens) is allowed. Three or four-course menus comprising appetizer, soup, fish, meat, vegetarian or surprise main course, dessert (three-course with choice between soup or dessert).

Zum Nussbaum
U S Alexanderplatz
Am Nussbaum 3
☎ 242 30 95
Daily from noon
[1]

This is the oldest restaurant in Berlin, founded in 1571 when the city was still called Cölln. It was destroyed in World War II but has been faithfully reconstructed down to the last detail. The satirical artist Heinrich Zille stayed here.

Zur letzten Instanz
U Klosterstrasse
Waisenstrasse 14–16
☎ 242 55 28
Mon–Sat noon–1am
[1]

Another claimant to the title of oldest establishment in Berlin, this typical pub offers good local cuisine.

POTSDAMER PLATZ

Lindenbräu im Sony Center
U S Potsdamer Platz
Bellevuestrasse 3–5
☎ 25 75 12 80
Daily 11am–1am
[1]

A combination of Bavarian cosiness and contemporary architecture. Home-brewed "white beer" and hearty portions of South German specialities, best enjoyed on the roof terrace.

Lutter & Wegner im Weinhaus Huth
U S Potsdamer Platz
Alte Potsdamer Strasse 5
☎ 25 29 43 50
Daily 11am–midnight
[2]

Small and comfortable restaurant overlooking Potsdamer Platz, specializing in German and Austrian cuisine. Excellent wines.

Salomon Bagels
U S Potsdamer Platz

Alte Potsdamer Strasse 7
Arkaden, 1st floor,
Shop 102
☎ 25 29 76 26
Mon–Sat 9am–9pm,
Sun 10–7pm
[1]

For a delicious snack with a view over the Arcades, go to the upper floor to find Solomon's fresh bagels in many variations: plain, with poppyseeds or sesame seeds, cream cheese or salmon.

TIERGARTEN

Ambrosius
Ⓤ Nollendorfplatz
Einemstrasse 14
☎ 264 05 26
Mon–Fri 8am–midnight,
Sat, Sun from 9am
[1]

The menu features traditional German specialities.

Angkor Wat
Ⓢ Bellevue
Paulstrasse 22
☎ 393 39 22
Mon–Fri 6pm–midnight,
Sat, Sun noon–midnight
Reservation preferred
[1]

Tasty Cambodian cuisine, fish and vegetarian dishes.

Brewbaker
Ⓢ Bellevue
Flensburger Strasse 415
☎ 39 90 51 56
Mon–Fri 2–11pm,
Sat, Sun 4–11pm
[1]

Under the red-brick railway arch of S-Bahn Bellevue station, a gourmet brasserie serving several varieties of home-brewed beers as well as open wines from famous German vineyards.

Capt'n Schillow
Ⓤ Ernst-Reuter-Platz
Ⓢ Tiergarten
Strasse des 17. Juni
Am Charlottenburger Tor
☎ 31 50 50 15
Mon–Fri noon–midnight,
Sat, Sun 10am–11pm
[1]

Restaurant on a barge on the Landwehr canal. Fish dishes, both local and international recipes. Sun deck.

Hugos
ⓊⓈ Zoologischer Garten
Hotel Intercontinental
Budapester Strasse 2
☎ 26 02 12 63
Mon–Sat from 6pm
(food served till 10.30pm)
[4]

Prestigious French cuisine in an extremely chic setting on the 14th floor of the Intercontinental Hotel, with an incomparable view of Berlin.

Paris–Moskau
Ⓢ Hauptbahnhof
Alt-Moabit 141
☎ 394 20 81
Daily 6pm–around midnight, Mon–Fri also noon–3pm
[2]

Take a detour up to the working-class district of Moabit for a great culinary experience: excellent fish and seafood dishes, and around 240 wines in this small half-timbered building dating from 1898, near the railway line linking Paris and Moscow.

CHARLOTTENBURG

Alcatraz
Ⓢ Bundesplatz
Bundesplatz 6
☎ 853 46 54
Mon–Thurs from 4pm,

Salomon Bagels

Fri, Sat from noon (food served to midnight)

People are happy to do time in this Mexican restaurant. The food is excellent, the atmosphere irresistible, and there are more than 100 cocktails to whet your appetite.

Amrit III
U Victoria-Luise-Platz
Winterfeldstrasse 40
Schöneberg
☎ 21 01 46 40
Daily noon–1am

A branch of the well-known Indian restaurants that have made names for themselves in Kreuzberg (Oranienstrasse 202–203) and Mitte (Oranienburger Strasse 45). Typical music and large portions.

Biscotti
U Wilmersdorfer Strasse
Pestalozzistrasse 88
☎ 312 39 37
Mon–Sat 6pm–half past midnight

Mamma mia! Handmade pasta, a small but exquisite selection of high-quality Italian dishes.

Café im Literaturhaus-Wintergarten
U Uhlandstrasse
Fasanenstrasse 23
☎ 882 54 14
Daily 9.30am–1am

Very elegant café and winter garden, with an attractive garden setting beneath the trees in summer. Poetry readings sometimes take place (it's above a lovely bookshop).

Café Savigny
S Savignyplatz
Grolmanstrasse 53–54
☎ 44 70 83 86
Daily 9am–midnight

A friendly and stylish little café frequented by intellectuals and artists. Excellent breakfast, served till 4pm.

Dicke Wirtin
S Savignyplatz
Carmerstrasse 9
☎ 312 49 52
Daily from noon

A traditional pub named after the "fat landlady" who once ran it—she was loved for her kind heart and hearty stews. Nowadays you can still dine on stews or other Berlin specialities such as meatballs, dumplings with green and red cabbage or even bread and dripping *(Schmalzstulle)*.

Dicker Wirt
S Westend
Danckelmannstrasse 43
☎ 321 99 42
Daily 3pm–4am (food served till midnight)

A typical dimly lit Berlin pub serving reasonably priced food.

Don Quijote
S Savignyplatz
Bleibtreustrasse 41
☎ 881 32 08
Daily 4pm–1am

The leading Spanish restaurant in Berlin. Tapas and tasty main dishes. Olé!

Florian
S Savignyplatz
Grolmanstrasse 52
☎ 313 91 84
Daily 6pm–3am

Dicke Wirtin

The southern German specialities served in this restaurant have a refined French accent. A meeting point for film folks during the Berlinale.

Ho Lin Wah
U Kurfürstendamm
Kurfürstendamm 218
☎ 882 11 71
Daily noon–midnight
1

Chinese restaurant in the covered passage, serving delicious *dim sum*, with generous portions.

Khayyam
U Adenauerplatz
Damaschkestrasse 17
☎ 216 47 47
Daily except Mon noon–11pm
1

Named after the Persian poet Omar Khayyam, this restaurant serves dishes from Iran and the Near East. Belly dancing on Saturdays.

Mar y Sol
S Savignyplatz
Savignyplatz 5
☎ 313 25 93
Daily 11.30am–midnight, Fri, Sat to 1am
2

Chic restaurant with a lovely summer terrace; Spanish dishes and an excellent, varied tapas buffet, near the Ku'damm.

Marjellchen
S Savignyplatz
Mommsenstrasse 9
☎ 883 26 76
Daily 5–11.30pm
2

A GERMAN MENU

Typical starters include *Hackepeter*, the local version of steak tartare, and *Soleier*, hard-boiled eggs pickled in brine and eaten with Berlin mustard, *Mostrich*.

Fish comes fresh from the Havel. Try *Havelaal grün*, eel in dill sauce, or *Havelzander*, pikeperch, with *Salzkartoffeln*, tasty boiled potatoes. If you have a hearty appetite and no vegetarian tendencies, tackle the supreme Berlin delicacy *Eisbein mit Sauerkraut und Erbsenpüree*—pig's knuckle on a purée of peas with sauerkraut.

A popular sweet is *Rote Grütze* (a compote of raspberries, cherries and blackcurrants).

Otherwise, Berliners happily tuck into a generous slice of *Schwarzwälder Kirschtorte*, the creamy layered cherry and chocolate gateau from the Black Forest.

DRINKS

The top German wines are considered to be the Riesling wines of the Rheingau. But Berlin's most popular drink remains beer. It is served *vom Fass*, on tap, or bottled, in these varieties: Export, light and smooth; Pils, light and very dry; and Bock, dark and rich. You will see Berliners drinking a red or green liquid from large bowl-like glasses: that's *Berliner Weisse*, a very pale beer with a shot of raspberry (*mit Rot*) or woodruff syrup (*mit Grün*).

The food here is cooked from venerable old recipes handed down by the owner's East Prussian grandmother. Dishes include *Königsberger Klopse* (beef and pork meatballs with sardines and anchovies) and *Elchbraten* (roast venison). After all that you'll probably need a glass of Danziger Goldwasser (a clear, spicy spirit full of flittering flakes of gold) to get up from the table.

Meineke X
Ⓤ Kurfürstendamm
Meinekestrasse 10
☎ 882 31 58
Daily noon–1am
②

Café, restaurant and bistro where you can indulge in one of Berlin's best buffets and round off the meal with an old-fashioned schnaps.

Restaurant Leibniz-Klause
Ⓢ Savignyplatz
Mommsenstrasse 57 (entrance Leibnitzstrasse)
☎ 323 70 68
Daily noon–1am
②

Award-winning restaurant serving tasty Berlin specialities as well as international cuisine. Traditional bar with a cosy atmosphere.

Sachiko Sushi
Ⓤ Uhlandstrasse
Grolmanstrasse 47
☎ 313 22 82
Mon–Sat noon–midnight, Sun from 4pm
①

Popular sushi bar. Its Japanese name Sachicko means Child of Fortune.

Scarabeo
Ⓤ Uhlandstrasse
Ludwigkirchstrasse 6
Wilmersdorf
☎ 885 06 16
Daily 4pm–1am
①

Egyptian restaurant with good food, tea and pastries. Belly-dancing at the weekend, along with the hubble-bubble pipes.

Shima
Ⓤ Eisenacher Strasse
Schwäbische Strasse 5
Schöneberg
☎ 211 19 90
Daily from 6.30pm
②

Very stylish restaurant with laid-back lounge area; Asian cuisine, beautifully presented.

Weisser Elefant
Ⓤ Fehrbellinerplatz
Wegenerstrasse 1–2
Wilmersdorf

☎ 86 40 93 06
Mon–Fri 9am–10.30pm
[1]
Multi-faceted gastronomic cuisine, friendly atmosphere. No alcohol. Terrace in summer.

PRENZLAUER BERG

Café Chagall
U Senefelderplatz
Kollwitzstrasse 2
☎ 441 58 81
Daily from 10am
[1]

A cosy café serving Russian specialities; there's a fireplace to keep things warm, and sometimes live music.

Frida Kahlo
U Eberswalder Strasse
Lychener Strasse 37
☎ 445 70 16
Daily from 9am
[1]

Mexican specialities served in hearty portions. Frequented by young people. Several varieties of Mexican beer and tequila feature on the drinks menu.

Konnopke's Imbiss
U Eberswalder Strasse
Schönhauser Allee 44a
☎ 442 77 65
Mon–Fri 6am–8pm, Sat noon–7pm
[1]

Beneath the U-Bahn you'll find a snack bar serving the best curry sausage *(Currywurst)* in Berlin.

Nola's am Weinberg
U RosenthalerPlatz
Veteranenstrasse 9
☎ 44 04 07 66
Daily 10am–1am (food served till 11.30pm)
[1]

Popular Swiss restaurant serving traditional dishes. Large summer terrace with reclining chairs and a view over the Volkspark.

Ostwind
U Eberswalder Strasse
Husemannstrasse 13
☎ 441 59 51
Mon–Sat 6pm–midnight, Sun 11am–midnight
[1]

The East Wind brings authentic Chinese cuisine with the accent on wholesomeness.

Pasternak
U Senefelder Platz
Knaackstrasse 22–24
☎ 441 33 99
Daily 9am–1am
[1]

Excellent Russian specialities, and good lunches on weekdays. Spacious terrace.

Prater
U Eberswalder Strasse
Kastanienallee 7–9
☎ 448 56 88
Restaurant Mon–Sat from 6pm, Sun from noon (food served till 11pm, Fri, Sat to 11.30pm)
Biergarten: Apr–Sept in fine weather, daily from noon
[1]

Berlin's oldest and loveliest beer-garden, serving regional specialities and attracting a clientele of actors, artists and locals.

Trattoria Paparazzi
U Eberswalder Strasse
Husemannstrasse 35
☎ 440 73 33

KARTOFFELPUFFER

Every German region has its potato pancakes. Those of Berlin are known as *Kartoffelpuffer*. Besides the very proper High German and scarcely ever used *Kartoffelpfannkuchen*, they are known elsewhere as *Baggers, Bambis, Dätscher, Dotsch, Glitscher, Hatscheln, Kröbbelche, Pickat, Reibekuchen, Reibeplätzchen, Reiberdatschi, Rievkoche* and *Schepperlinge*. Not to mention Jewish *Latkes* and Swiss *Rösti*. If you are to believe the cooks, the dishes themselves, like the regional names, are each completely different. Anyway, the Berlin variety can be eaten with *Apfelmus*, a thick apple sauce, or *Sauerrahm* (sour cream)—or, for a real gourmet delight, with a dollop of each on either side, as an accompaniment for smoked salmon.

Kartoffelpuffer for six

1 kg potatoes
2 onions, finely chopped
2 eggs, beaten
100 g flour
salt, pinch of finely grated nutmeg, vegetable oil

1. Peel potatoes, and keep in cold water until you are ready to grate them.
2. Grate potatoes coarsely by hand; stir in the chopped onions. The mixture should be lumpy and not too creamy. Add beaten eggs. Sift in up to 100 g flour to make fairly liquid consistency, not too thick. Add salt and nutmeg.
3. Heat about 2 cm of vegetable oil in frying pan. When the oil is very hot, use a large soupspoon as a measure to put equal amounts of batter into the oil. Fry the pancakes on each side until they have turned brown and are crispy around the edges.
4. Drain the pancakes on paper towels placed on a large platter over a saucepan of simmering water, or keep them warm in the oven.

CITYBITES 109

Daily from 6pm (food served till 11.30pm)
2
Locals and businessmen get together in this Italian restaurant. Fresh food, good wines.

FRIEDRICHSHAIN

Sauerkraut und Bulgur
Ⓢ Ostbahnhof
Strasse der Pariser Kommune 35
☎ 29 77 36 31
Daily 11.30am–midnight
1
A varied menu ranging from German to Mediterranean dishes.

Volckswirtschaft
Ⓤ Ⓢ Warschauer Strasse
Krossener Strasse 17
☎ 69 20 68 61
Daily from 9am
1
Tasty dishes made from organic ingredients.

KREUZBERG

Bagdad
Ⓤ Schlesisches Tor
Schlesische Strasse 2
☎ 612 69 62
Daily 2pm–midnight
1
Turkish restaurant serving meat and fish grilled over charcoal. In the adjoining snack bar, open round the clock, you can buy Kreuzberg's best kebabs.

Henne
Ⓤ Kottbusser Tor
Leuschnerdamm 25
☎ 614 77 30
Tues–Sat from 7pm, Sun from 5pm
Reservation advised
1
The crispy half-chicken served in this typical old inn and beergarden has a cult following. They also serve potato or cabbage salad and meatballs. The interior is true to its charming 1907 origins.

Il Casolare
Ⓤ Schönleinstrasse
Grimmstrasse 30
☎ 69 50 66 10
Daily noon–midnight
1
Popular restaurant on the Landwehr canal, where you can find excellent pizzas and a typical Italian atmosphere. Wines served from the barrel, one red, one white.

Joe Peñas Cantina y Bar
Ⓤ Gneisaustrasse
Marheinekeplatz 3
☎ 693 60 44
Mon–Fri from noon, Sat, Sun from 9am (food served till midnight)
1
Popular, trendy place with exuberant décor and Mexican cuisine. Live music.

Le Cochon Bourgeois
Ⓤ Südstern
Fichtestrasse 24
☎ 693 01 01
Tues–Sat 6pm–1am
3
Exquisite French food, inventive yet not too pretentious, served in an elegant setting. Piano music. Extensive wine list.

Liebermanns im Jüdischen Museum
Ⓤ Hallesches Tor
Lindenstrasse 9–14
☎ 25 93 97 60
Daily 10am–8pm, Mon to 10pm
1
Delicacies from Israel and Mediterranean dishes in the museum restaurant, not exclusively kosher. The highlight of the week is the Monday evening Oriental Buffet (6–10pm) accompanied by live Klezmer music.

Sale e Tabacchi
Ⓤ Kochstrasse
Kochstrasse 18/Rudi-Dutschke-Strasse 23
☎ 252 11 55
Daily from 10am (food served till midnight)
1
The best of Bella Italia in the publishing district. Swiss architect Max Dudler converted the Rudi-Dutschke-Haus for this Italian restaurant.

cityNights

They say that Berlin never closes. For news of what's on, see *Tip and Zitty*, lively magazines appearing every two weeks, or the *Time Out* website: www.timeout.com/berlin
Berlin's long classical musical tradition attracts the world's finest performers to its grand concert halls, while three main opera houses maintain the city's reputation. Church music can be heard at the Berliner Dom and St Hedwig's Catholic cathedral. And musical comedy is still going strong—Berlin can claim to have invented the genre before the Americans made it their own. As for theatre, great classical and experimental drama still has a solid home in Berlin.

For theatre and musical events, you can book in advance through Berlin Tourismus Marketing, ☎ 25 00 25, the KaDeWe department store, ☎ 217 77 54, or try for last-minute discounts through Hekticket, Hardenbergstr. 29d (Bahnhof Zoo), or Karl-Liebknecht-Strasse 12 (Alexanderplatz), ☎ 230 99 30.

Staatsoper Unter den Linden

CLASSICAL MUSIC

Deutsche Oper Berlin
U Deutsche Oper
Bus 101, 109
Bismarckstrasse 35
Charlottenburg
☎ 343 84 343
Behind the gleaming façade of this 1960s glass and concrete building, Berlin's largest opera house produces a classical repertoire but also first performances of contemporary works.

Komische Oper Berlin
U Französische Strasse
Behrenstrasse 55–57
☎ 47 99 74 00
The Comic Opera presents classic and modern operas, operettas, children's opera and *(Musikmärchen)* in their German versions.

Konzerthaus Berlin
U Stadtmitte,
Französische Strasse
Gendarmenmarkt
☎ 203 09 21 01
In the four halls of the former Schauspielhaus, the home of the Berlin Konzerthaus orchestra, more than 550 performances are held every year, among them themed recitals with famous musicians from Germany and elsewhere.

Philharmonie
U S Potsdamer Platz
Herbert-von-Karajan-Strasse 1
Kulturforum
☎ 254 88 999
The home of the Berlin Philharmonic Orchestra. The Kammermusiksaal, next door, holds chamber music and solo recitals (same phone number).

Staatsoper Unter den Linden
U S Friedrichstrasse
Unter den Linden 7
☎ 20 35 45 55
The historic royal court opera house provides a splendid setting for international operas and ballet.

MUSICAL COMEDY AND VARIETY

Friedrichstadtpalast
U Oranienburger Tor
Friedrichstrasse 107
☎ 23 26 23 26
Large revue theatre with lavish performances, world-class dancers, singers and artistes.

Theater am Potsdamer Platz
U S Potsdamer Platz
Marlene-Dietrich-Platz 1
Ticket-Hotline:
018 05 44 44;
Information: 25 92 90
Musical theatre, and in February the main venue of the Berlinale international film festival.

Theater des Westens
U S Zoologischer Garten
Kantstrasse 12
Charlottenburg
☎ 018 05 44 44
This traditional theatre is one of the best addresses in Berlin for operettas and modern musicals.

THEATRE

Berliner Ensemble
U S Friedrichstrasse
Bertolt-Brecht-Platz 1
☎ 28 40 81 55
The neo-baroque Theater am Schiffbauerdamm, built in 1892, was the home of Bertolt Brecht's theatre company, the Berliner Ensemble, and opened for the 1928 premiere of *The Threepenny Opera*. It is now managed by Claus Peymann, who produces political theatre for modern times.

Deutsches Theater
U S Friedrichstrasse
Schumannstrasse 13a
☎ 28 44 12 25
Once directed by the legendary Max Reinhardt, the elegant DT is widely considered to be Berlin's most beautiful venue. Behind the classical façade are two adjoining stages, the main one originally used for operettas and now generally used for classic drama, and the smaller Kammerspiele for modern plays. The repertory company of 40 actors produce up to 20 new productions per season. In the lobby, the newly founded Box presents young contemporary writers.

English Theatre Berlin (ETB)
U Platz der Luftbrücke
Fidicinstrasse 40
☎ 691 1211
Founded in 1990 as The Friends of the Italian Opera, the theatre hosts visting companies in a new venue opened in 2006.

Komödie und Theater am Kurfürstendamm
U Uhlandstrasse
Kurfürstendamm 206–209
Charlottenburg
☎ 88 59 11 88
Light comedy and vaudeville.

Maxim-Gorki-Theater
U S Friedrichstrasse
Am Festungsgraben 2
☎ 20 22 11 15
Built to a design by Karl Friedrich Schinkel in 1825–27, this large theatre has two stages: the main one used for classical drama, the smaller, "rehearsal" stage for contemporary plays.

Renaissance-Theater
U Ernst-Reuter-Platz
Hardenbergstrasse 6
Charlottenburg
☎ 312 42 02
The beautiful 1920s Art Deco theatre presents contemporary drama and comedy appealing to a wide audience.

Schaubühne am Lehniner Platz
U Adenauerplatz
Kurfürstendamm 153
Charlottenburg
☎ 89 00 23
Experimental and contemporary theatre with a critical look at the problems of modern society.

Volksbühne
U Rosa-Luxemburg-Platz
Rosa-Luxemburg-Platz
☎ 24 06 57 77
The "People's Theatre" was built in 1913–14 with the aim of promoting social-realist plays of the day at prices accessible to the common worker. It now has a reputation as one of the most provocative and experimental theatres in Germany.

CABARET

Bar Jeder Vernunft
U Spichernstrasse
Schaperstrasse 24
Charlottenburg
☎ 883 15 82
Musical comedies (for instance Cabaret) are performed in the exquisite setting of an Art Nouveau tent decked out in mirrors and red velvet.

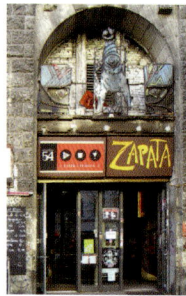

Café Zapata

Die Stachelschweine
U S Zoologischer Garten
Europa-Center
Tauentzienstrasse
9–12 Charlottenburg
☎ 261 47 95
You'll need to understand German as well as Berlin's scathing sense of humour to appreciate this prickliest of cabarets (the name means Porcupine). In the basement of the Europa-Center.

Die Wühlmäuse
U Theodor-Heuss-Platz
Pommernallee 2–4
Charlottenburg
☎ 30 67 30 11
In the modernist 1920s Amerikahaus, this legendary cabaret was founded by Dieter Hallervorden 40 years ago; shows are mainly satiric commentaries of political themes.

Distel
U S Friedrichstrasse
Friedrichstrasse 101
☎ 204 47 04
Entertaining political satire in what was the most famous cabaret of East Germany.

BARS

Bar am Lützowplatz
U Nollendorfplatz
Lützowplatz 7
☎ 262 68 07
Barmen in white dinner jackets behind Berlin's longest and narrowest bar cater to the chic clientèle. Great choice of cocktails, malt whiskies and champagne; noisy, crowded atmosphere, with jazz, electro and global beat.

Café Zapata
U Oranienburger Tor
Oranienburger Strasse 54–56a
☎ 281 61 09
With an interior designed by artists from nearby galleries and studios, bare walls, barbed wire, tin cans and other trash, not to mention a flame-throwing dragon over the bar, this is a popular alternative hangout.

Harry's New York Bar
U Nollendorfplatz
Lützuwfer 15

Hotel Esplanade
☎ 254 78 86 33
Live music Monday to Saturday in an exclusive hotel bar that stays lively till the early hours.

Kaffee Burger
U Rosa-Luxemburg-Platz
Torstrasse 60
☎ 28 04 64 95
A crazy club with gilded flowery wallpaper, famous for its bi-monthly Russian disco, with events ranging from poetry and short-story readings to films and live music.

Newton Bar
U Französische Strasse
Charlottenstrasse 57
☎ 20 29 540
Cool atmosphere and cosmopolitan clientèle; first-class cocktails. Photos by Helmut Newton on the walls, and on the first floor stands Berlin's biggest humidor.

Schwarzes Café
S Savignyplatz
Kantstrasse 48
Charlottenburg
☎ 313 80 38
Open round the clock, this is the place where clubbers come for breakfast after a night on the town.

Valentin Stüberl
U Rathaus Neukölln

Donaustrasse 112
Neukölln
☎ 17 13 22 89 42
Among the many counter-cultural venues in Neukölln, the Valentin Stüberl, named after the Bavarian comedian Karl Valentin, is a lively venue with a varied cultural programme tending towards political satire (and a small menu of Bavarian specialities).

Würgeengel
🚇 Kottbusser Tor
Dresdener Strasse 122
Kreuzberg
☎ 615 55 60
The "Exterminating Angel" is a cosy bar with red velvet, gilt-edged mirrors and stucco, attracting a varied clientèle. Excellent *tapas*.

Zosch
🚇 Oranienburger Strasse
Tucholskystrasse 30
☎ 280 76 64
A pleasant alternative bar on the first floor serving delectable snacks; concerts and other performances in the basement.

LIVE MUSIC

A-Trane
🚇 Savignyplatz
Bleibtreustrasse 1/Ecke Pestalozzistrasse
Charlottenburg
☎ 313 25 50
Jazz of all kinds played by national and international stars, in a pleasant atmosphere.

Junction Bar
🚇 Gneisenaustrasse
Gneisenaustrasse 18
Kreuzberg
☎ 694 66 02
Live music every evening: jazz, blues, funk soul, rap and more.

Kalkscheune
🚇 Oranienburger Strasse
Johannisstrasse 2
☎ 59 00 43 40
Apart from concerts, parties are organized on different themes, such as "Fish seeking bicycle" (for singles).

CABARET

Being naturally irreverent, caustic and witty, Berliners have made satirical cabaret, particularly of the political variety, their own art form. After a period of stagnation, the targets of its satirical barbs are back in town with the national government moving from Bonn to Berlin in 1999.

Cabaret's golden era was the 1920s. The Schall und Rauch (Noise and Smoke) club in Max Reinhardt's Grosses Schauspielhaus theatre attracted Berlin's top creative talents. Photomontage artist John Heartfield and painter George Grosz designed the programme. Political commentator Kurt Tucholsky collaborated with poets Klabund and Walter Mehring to write mordant songs and sketches. Among the star singers were Claire Waldoff, Marlene Dietrich and Trude Hesterberg, the latter using a fellow named Bert Brecht to write her songs—he was unknown at the time.

Knaack-Klub
U Rosa-Luxemburg-Platz
Greifswalder Strasse 224
Prenzlauer Berg
☏ 442 70 60
The cornerstone of Berlin clubs. Live music and disco, "Alternative", Indie and R'n'B. Billiards and karaoke in the Dizzy Lounge.

Frannz
U Eberswalder Strasse
Schönhauser Allee 36
Prenzlauer Berg
☏ 72 62 79 333
Every evening, artists of the new generation and nonconformist musicians representing every style perform on stage.

Quasimodo
U S Zoologischer Garten
Kantstrasse 12a
Charlottenburg
☏ 312 80 86
Famous jazz club that also lends its stage to funk, soul, Latina and blues.

CLUBS

Adagio
U Potsdamer Platz
Marlene-Dietrich-Platz 1
☏ 25 89 890
Chic disco with an absolutely sumptuous interior, a meeting place for the well-heeled.

Alte Kantine in der Kulturbrauerei
U Eberswalder Strasse
Knaackstrasse 97
Prenzlauer Berg
☏ 44 31 50
Cool atmosphere, big dance floors and golden oldies from the days of rock and pop.

Clärchens Ballhaus
S Oranienburger Strasse
Auguststrasse 24
☏ 282 92 95
People of all ages get together for salsa, tango, swing and waltz in a 1920s atmosphere.

Grüner Salon
U Rosa-Luxemburg-Platz
Volksbühne
Rosa-Luxemburg-Platz
☏ 28 59 89 36
Smart salon atmosphere, with mirrors and oak floors. Concerts and special theme evenings: salsa, tango and swing.

Icon
U Eberswalder Strasse
Cantianstrasse 15
Prenzlauer Berg
☏ 32 29 70 520
In the cellars of a former brewery, dance to the beat of drum and bass, hip-hop and reggae.

Maria am Ostbahnhof
S Ostbahnhof
An der Schillingbrücke/
Stralauer Platz 33–34
Friedrichshain
☏ 21 23 81 90
A mixed audience comes here to dance to trendy electronic sounds.

Oxymoron
S Hackescher Markt
Rosenthaler Strasse 40–41
Main Entrance on Hackesche Höfe
☏ 23 39 18 86
The elegant coffee house and restaurant undergoes a transformation Tues, Fri and Sat when it becomes a smart nightclub.

Soda Club
U Eberswalder Strasse
Schönhauser Allee 36
Prenzlauer Berg
☏ 44 31 51 55
Smart disco in the Kulturbrauerei, with mostly black music, salsa and house.

Watergate
U Schlesisches Tor
Falckensteinstrasse 49
Kreuzberg
☏ 61 28 03 96
If you can persuade the doormen to let you in, you can dance to electro, house, drum and bass or funk, pausing now and then to drink in the magnificent view over the Spree and the Oberbaum bridge.

BERLIN ON THE SCREEN

Berlin's Max and Emil Skladanowsky presented the world's first public film-show on November 1, 1895 at the Wintergarten music hall on Friedrichstrasse—eight weeks before the better publicized event staged by the Lumière brothers in Paris. Their Bioscop was technically inferior to the Frenchmen's cinematograph, but Berlin soon became the most prolific and creative film centre in Europe. With studios in Berlin-Tempelhof and Potsdam-Babelsberg, the UFA production company's mass-market films rivalled Hollywood throughout the 1920s. For those who saw cinema as an art form, Berlin was producing such Expressionist works as Robert Wiene's *Cabinet of Dr Caligari* and Friedrich Wilhelm Murnau's *Nosferatu*. And in many films of the past century, both commercial and artistic, the vibrant city of Berlin itself has been a major star attraction.

In 1951, the Berlin International Film Festival, also called the Berlinale, was founded. Since 1978 it has been held every February, and has become one of the most important events on the international film industry's calendar. Some 20 films compete for the main awards, the Golden Bear for the best motion picture and lifetime achievement, and the Silver Bear for the best actor, actress, screenplay, music, and so on.

The 1920s

Even before studios ventured into the city for location shooting, the light and shadow of Berlin in the 1920s provided a perfect inspirational backdrop for the brilliance and squalor of their films. Both came to the fore when UFA's Babelsberg studios recreated a glittering Berlin shopping street for Joe May's *Asphalt* (1928), an erotic crime thriller starring Betty Amann as a seduc-

tive jewel thief. Murnau's darker *Der letzte Mann* (translated as *The Last Laugh*, 1924) portrays the wretched fate of a chief porter in a grand hotel (modelled on the Adlon on Unter den Linden) losing his splendid gold-braided uniform and self-respect when demoted to toilet-attendant. In Fritz Lang's science fiction extravaganza *Metropolis* (1927), many see its inspiration in the unbridled and dehumanizing urban sprawl of Berlin itself. Alfred Döblin's classical novel of the city's 1920s underworld, *Berlin Alexanderplatz*, has twice been filmed (by Phil Jutzi in 1931 and Rainer Werner Fassbinder for television in 1980) to portray the grim atmosphere of backstreet tenements in Prenzlauer Berg and the old Jewish Scheunenviertel.

Third Reich
The advent of Adolf Hitler drove Berlin's major cinema talents to Hollywood, including directors like Ernst Lubitsch, George Wilhelm Pabst, Fritz Lang and Billy Wilder, but also actors Peter Lorre and Marlene Dietrich. Those who stayed produced second-rate propaganda, except for actress-turned-director Leni Riefenstahl whose propaganda was first-rate. Her *Olympia* documentary of Berlin's 1936 Olympic Games set the creative standard for generations of sports filming. The focus on idealized physical beauty promoted Hitler's ideology of "Aryan supremacy" while fudging its underlying ugly racism.

Cold War
After World War II, Hollywood came to Berlin. In 1961, just before the Berlin Wall made it less of a joke, director Billy Wilder came "home" to

make *One, Two, Three*. His often outrageous comedy, with James Cagney as a Coca Cola salesman embroiled in east-west intrigues in Berlin, takes pot shots at Communist and capitalist hypocrisy—and German "war guilt", too. Martin Ritt's *Spy Who Came In from the Cold* (1965) films John LeCarré's very cold and cynical look at the Cold War on both sides of the Wall. In *Octopussy* (1983), James Bond got into the act with Roger Moore foiling the enemies of the free world at Checkpoint Charlie. For a German view of the city in the years before the Wall came down, Fassbinder's *Die dritte Generation* (*The Third Generation*, 1979) is an uncompromising look at the ambiguities of leftist revolutionaries in West Berlin seeking social justice through acts of terrorism. Wim Wenders' enigmatic *Der Himmel über Berlin* (*Wings of Desire*, 1986) films—unknowingly—the last days of the divided city with its bleak no-man's land along the western side of the Wall, visited by a couple of fallen angels, Bruno Ganz and Peter Falk.

Since 1989

The newly reunified and reconstructed city provided Berlin's regenerated cinema of the 1990s with exciting and photogenic locations. The point was made explicitly with director Wolfgang Becker's *Das Leben ist eine Baustelle* (*Life is all you get*, 1997) in which bulldozers and cement-mixers seem to be major players in the life confronting a new generation of Berliners. Similarly, in Tom Tykwer's *Lola rennt* (*Run, Lola, Run*, 1998), new buildings emerging from the city's battered old neighbourhoods are the backdrop for flaming red-haired Franka Potente's 20-minute race to save her boyfriend. The worldwide success *Goodbye Lenin* (2003), also by Wolfgang Becker, is a hilarious and poignant picture of East Berliners' difficult adjustment to their unfamiliar freedoms after the Wall came down. By 2005, post-war German cinema could at last confront Hitler's Berlin, with Oliver Hirschbiegel's *Der Untergang* (*Downfall*) portraying the Führer's final days in his bunker—with the street-scenes of the Russian assault shot, ironically, in St Petersburg. The German capital was once again just a metropolis with its dose of big city alienation, sensitively portrayed in Christian Petzold's *Gespenster* (*Ghosts*). Or the everyday craziness of Dani Levy's *Alles auf Zucker* (*Go For Zucker*), a, yes, Jewish family comedy. On film at least, Berlin had become a *normal* town.

cityFacts

Airports	122
Bicycle hire	122
Boat tours	122
Climate	123
Clothing	123
Communications	123
Customs Controls	123
Disabled Visitors	124
Driving	124
Emergencies	124
Formalities	125
Health	125
Languages	125
Lost and Found	125
Media	125
Money	126
Opening hours	126
Public Holidays	126
Public Transport	126
Security	127
Taxis	128
Time difference	128
Tipping	128
Toilets	128
Tourist Information	128
Voltage	128

Airports
Berlin has two airports, both on ☎ 0180 5000 186. However, Tegel airport is due to close once Schönefeld opens as Berlin Brandenburg International.

Berlin-Tegel, 8 km (5 miles) northwest of the city centre, is still the busiest of the two airports. Buses X9 and 109 go to Zoologischer Garten, while JetExpressBus TXL links the airport to the administrative district.

Berlin-Schönefeld, 22 km (14 miles) east of the centre, is undergoing expansion to become the city's principal airport. To reach the centre you can take the Airport Express at Schönfeld Station (linked by bus from the airport, or a 5-minute walk) to Bahnhof Zoo, bus 171 to U-Bahn station Rudow, line 7; or S-Bahn line 9 via Alexanderplatz to Bahnhof Zoo.

Bicycle Hire
Berlin is flat, and the traffic is not too dense, so it is easy to get around on a bike. Guided tours are organized by Berlin on Bike
Knaackstrasse 97, Prenzlauer Berg
www.berlinonbike.de
☎ 43 73 99 99

You can hire a bike from several stations *(Fahrradstation)*:
Leipziger Strasse 56
Auguststrasse 29a
Friedrichstrasse 95 (entrance Dorotheenstrasse 30)
Goethestrasse 46, Charlottenburg
Kollwitzstrasse 77, Prenzlauerberg
Bergmannstrasse 9, Kreuzberg
www.fahrradstation.com
0180 510 80 00

Boat Tours
On a fine day, why not take a city tour or a 1 to 4-hour round-trip under the bridges on the Spree and Landwehrkanal. Departure points for the Reederei Riedel boats are Hansabrücke, Kottbusser Brücke, Corneliusbrücke, Märkisches Ufer, Moltkebrücke, Haus der Kulturen der Welt.

www.reederei-riedel.de
☎ 61 65 79 30.
Another company, Stern und Kreisschifffahrt organizes river cruises from dozens of departure points in Berlin and in Brandenburg;
www.sternundkreis.de
☎ 536 36 00

Climate
Berlin has a healthy continental climate, well known among Germans for the bracing quality of its air. Winters are crisp and cold, with the city's lakes and canals often freezing over for New Year's Day skating parties. Summers are warm, at times very hot, but not humid and so never stifling. Westerly winds bring showers in spring and autumn, but they rarely last long.

Clothing
Berlin's climate demands really warm clothing outside the spring and summer seasons, and a sweater (for cool evenings) and rainwear all year round. Otherwise, clothing should be light—in summer, cottons are less sticky than synthetics. Good walking shoes are essential.

Communications
Call worldwide with telecards from street-phones. The international dialling code to Germany is 49, and Berlin's city code is 30.

Post your mail for countries outside Germany in the slot marked *Andere Richtungen*. Most post offices open Mon–Sat 8am–6pm, Sat 8am–1pm. You can send e-mails and faxes from here. Main branches:

Joachimsthaler Strasse (Bahnhof Zoo/Kaufhaus Karstadt)
Mon–Sat 9am–8pm
Georgenstrasse 12 post office (Mitte)
Mon–Fri 6am–10pm, Sat, Sun from 8am

Customs Controls
These are minimal at point of entry. Residents of European Union countries may import a reasonable quantity of goods for personal use bought or acquired inside the EU but not at a duty-free shop. People from outside the

EU are entitled to a duty-free allowance of 200 cigarettes or 100 cigarillos or 50 cigars or 250 g of tobacco, 1 litre of spirits (exceeding 22%) and 2 litres of distilled beverages (less than 22%) and 2 litres of wine.

Disabled Visitors

In recent years, the Berlin authorities have made a great effort to provide good facilities for handicapped people. The transport network (BVG) and S-Bahn have transformed many of the buses, trains and stations to make them wheelchair-accessible. A free help service for ticket purchase, changing lines or vehicles operates from Monday to Friday 9am–7pm. You have to book at least a day ahead on tel. 25 41 44 14. Cinemas, theatres and shopping centres have also installed ramps and other facilities for easy access, and restaurants, supermarkets, museums and toilets that can be used by handicapped persons are indicated by a sign with a white arrow on a yellow background, and the words "Berlin barrierefrei".
Information service:
  Mobidat
  www.mobidat.net
  ☎ 74 77 71 15.

Driving

Berlin suffers from the same traffic snarls as any other European metropolis, but it does have good Autobahns and broad straight highways to get you fast to the outlying suburbs, woods and lakes. Parking in the city centre is a real problem, so keep your car only for longer trips.

Seat-belts are compulsory, and children under 12 must sit in the back of the car. Speed limits: motorway 130 kph (80 mph); country highways 100 kph (60 mph) and in town 50 kph (30 mph). Some sections of the motorway may have lower limits: watch out for the signs. Parking in town is permitted only in marked zones. Lead-free petrol is *bleifrei*.

Emergencies

Consular help is there only for critical situations, lost passports or worse, not for lost cash or tickets.
  Police 110, fire brigade 112.

Duty doctor ☎ (030) 31 00 31
Dental emergencies ☎ (030) 89 00 43 33.

Formalities
At your port of entry, a valid passport is all that most of you will need—just an identity card for members of EC countries. No special health certificates are required for European or North American citizens.

Health
Residents of EU countries benefit from a reciprocal health agreement (in case of emergency), as long as they have a European Health Insurance Card. Doctors, dentists and hospital staff are of generally good standard, many speaking English. If you anticipate need of prescription medicines, take your own as you may not find the exact equivalent on the spot.

Languages
Many but by no means all Germans speak some English, particularly the young generation. However, people will be pleasantly surprised if you greet them with a couple of words in their language. A *Guten Tag* (good morning) or *Guten Abend* (good evening), *Bitte* (please), *Danke* (thanks), *Bitte schön* (don't mention it) and *Auf Wiedersehen* are always welcome.

Lost and Found
The head office for found objects is:
   Platz der Luftbrücke 6, Tempelhof
   ☎ 75 60 31 01
If you lose something in the S-Bahn or in a bus, try calling at the
   BVG-Fundbüro
   Potsdamerstrasse 180, Schöneberg
   U Bülowstrasse or Kleistpark
   ☎ 19 449

Media
European newspapers, the International Herald Tribune and European edition of the *Wall Street Journal* arrive on the date of publication.

Hotels have cable and satellite TV with several English and American programmes.

Money
The Euro, divided into 100 cents. Coins: 1, 2, 5, 10, 20 and 50 cents, 1 and 2 euros; banknotes: 5, 10, 20, 50, 100, 200 and 500 euros.

Opening hours
Banks. Generally open Monday to Friday 9am–4pm (Tuesday and Thursday to 7pm). Some also open Saturday 9am–2pm.
Shops. Most shops open Monday to Saturday 10am–8pm, but they can choose their own opening hours between 6am and 8pm and are allowed to open several Sundays a year. In stations and airports, bakeries and other shops open on Sunday.
Museums and monuments. Hours vary. Enquire at your hotel or at the Tourist Office.
Post Office. The branch at Joachimstaler Strasse 7 (Bahnhof Zoo/Kaufhaus Karstadt) is open Monday to Saturday 9am–8pm. In Mitte, the post office at Georgenstrasse 12 opens Monday to Friday 6am–10pm, Saturday and Sunday from 8am; the other branches open Monday to Friday 8am–6pm, Saturday 8am–1pm.

Public Holidays
Jan 1	Neujahr (New Year)
May 1	Tag der Arbeit (Labour Day)
Oct 3	Tag der Einheit (Unification Day)
Dec 25	Weihnachten (Christmas)
Dec. 26	Stephanstag (St Stephen's Day)

Moveable:
Ascension Day, Whit Monday, Good Friday, Easter Monday

Public Transport
The city's BVG network (www.bvg.de) has a fast and efficient service of buses and city trains—subway (U-Bahn, **U**) and elevated (S-Bahn, **Tram**). For maps, information and special tourist tickets visit the Customer Centre:

Kundenzentrum, Holzmarkstrasse 14
🚇 🚊 Jannowitzbrücke
Other branches at Bahnhof Zoo and on Alexanderplatz.
Telephone information: ☎ 030 194 49, round the clock.

Tickets. There are special deals for tourists:

The Berlin WelcomeCard gives unlimited access to all Berlin buses and trains (zones A and B), as well as discounts of up to 50 per cent on more than 130 tourist attractions: €16.50 for 48 hours, €21.50 for 72 hours.

The Berlin and Potsdam WelcomeCard (€18 for 48 hours, €24.50 for 72 hours) is valid for one adult and up to three children under 14 for zones A, B and C (including Potsdam).

The CityTourCard gives unlimited access to all public transport within zones A and B and discounts for over 50 touristic sights (€15.90 for 48 hours, €20.50 for 72 hours); a similar card for three zones costs €17.50 for 48 hours, €23 for 72 hours.

A single ticket *(Einzelfahrschein)*, valid 2 hours, costs €2.10 for zones AB, and €2.80 for zones A, B and C.

Day tickets *(Tageskarte, €6.10 for two zones, €6.50 for three)* and the 7-day ticket *(7-Tage-Karte, €26.20 for two zones, €32.30 for three)* are all interchangeable on all BVG trains and buses. Three-zone cards are valid for one adult and up to three children. Children under 6 travel free, under 14 at a reduced rate *(Ermässigungstarif)*.

You can buy tickets from machines in all stations, at all the sales points with the BVG sign, in the trams and buses, and at most hotel reception desks. If you buy tickets in advance, you must validate them when you enter the tram or bus. Before you use the U- or S-Bahn, validate your ticket in the machine on the platform.

Trains. U-Bahn trains run every three to five minutes, all round the clock. S-Bahn trains run about every ten minutes.

Buses. Mostly double-decker, with frequent service and good late-night buses on main cross-town routes. The city is also served by trams.

Security
Pickpockets may be active in buses and trains. Without undue paranoia, don't tempt them with a wallet in the hip pocket or an open handbag.

Leave important documents and valuables in the hotel safe. Bahnhof Zoo still attracts some unsavoury characters. At night it's best to avoid the U-Bahn and S-Bahn stations at Friedrichstrasse and Alexanderplatz.

Taxis
There are taxi stands at all important crossroads, but you can also hail them in the street. The call centres are:
- ☎ 21 02 02
- ☎ 26 10 26
- ☎ 43 33 22
- ☎ 800 222 22 55

Time difference
Germany keeps Central European Time (CET), GMT+1 in winter and GMT+2 in summer for Daylight Saving Time. So it is one hour ahead of Great Britain, all year round.

Tipping
Service is included in restaurant and hotel bills, shared among the staff, but an extra 5 or 10 per cent is customary.

Toilets
The women's room is generally signposted *Damen* and the men's *Herren*. Public toilets are usually immaculate, but if you use the facilities in a bar or restaurant, it is customary to order at least a drink there.

Tourist Information
Before leaving home, take a look at the Tourist Offfice website:
www.visitBerlin.de
BERLIN Infostores are set up at Neues Kranzler Eck (Kurfürstendamm 21/Passage); Brandenburg Gate (Pariser Platz, south wing); Hauptbahnhof (Europa Platz 1, ground floor); ALEXA department store (near Alexanderplatz, Grunerstrasse 20); Reichstag (Berlin Pavillon/Scheidemannstrasse). Bookings and information by phone on +49/(0)30250025.

Voltage
Electric current is 220-volt 50-cycle AC; take an adaptor.

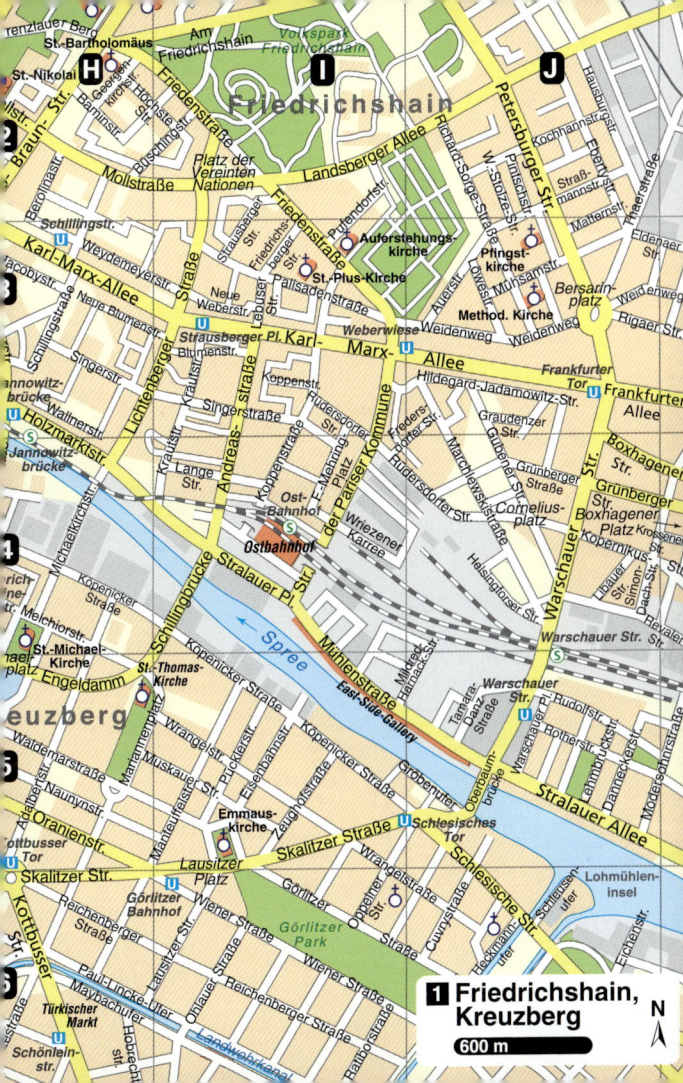

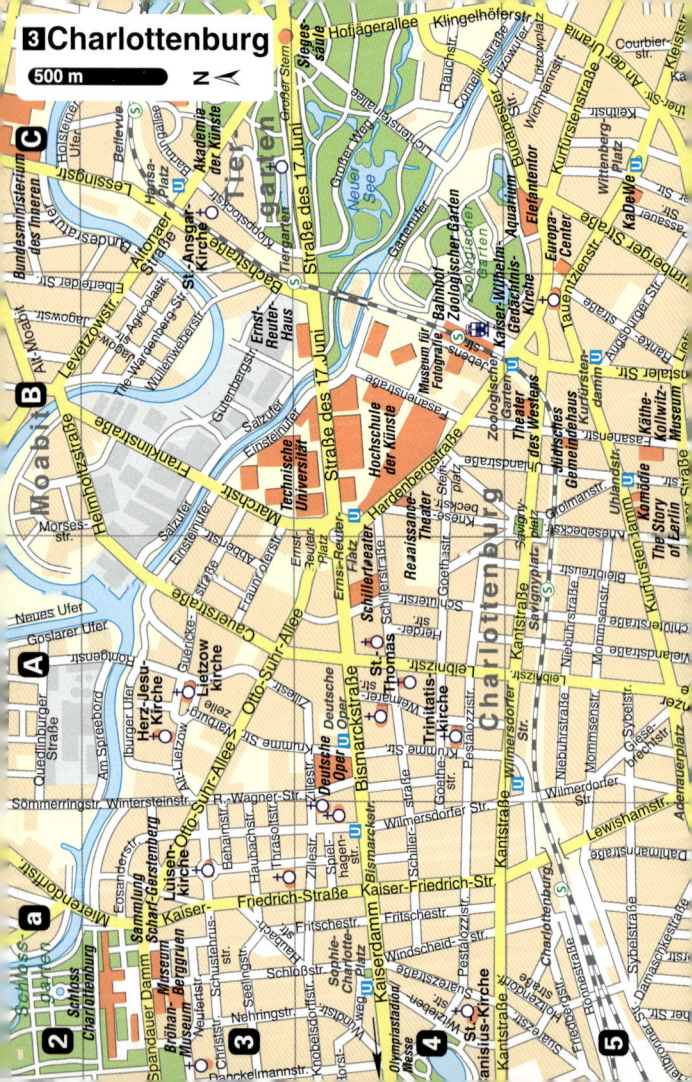

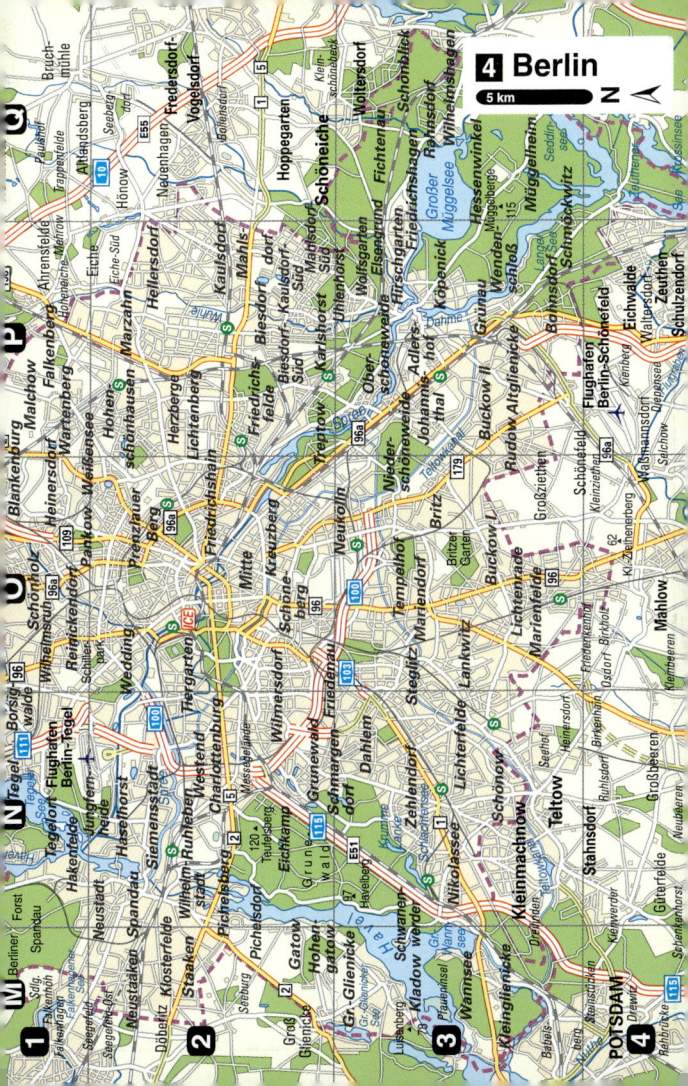

134 INDEX

Alexanderplatz 42
Alte Bibliothek 26, 34
Alte Nationalgalerie 31
Altes Museum 31
Ampelmann 85
Anhalter Bahnhof 51, 52
AquaDom and Sea Life 39–40
Bahnhof Zoo 61
Band des Bundes 63
Bankhaus Löbbecke 76
Bauhaus-Archiv 59–60
Bauspielplatz 66
Bebelplatz 26–27, 34
Bergmannstrasse 83
Berlin Philharmonic Orchestra 37
Berlin Wall 52, 54–55
Berlin Wall History Mile 54
Berliner Dom 29
Berliner Ensemble 113
Berliner Rathaus 40, 42
Berlinische Galerie 84
Bode-Museum 31
Bonbonmacherei Kolbe & Stecher 67
Botanischer Garten 90
Brandenburg Gate 22–23, 34
British Embassy 34
Bröhan-Museum 74
Brücke-Museum 91
Buchwald Konditorei 64
Bundeskanzleramt 63, 64
Bundespräsidialamt 64
Bundesschlange 64
Café Savigny 76
Checkpoint Charlie 54–55

Chinese Embassy 42
Dahlem 90–91
– Museums 90–91
debis-Haus 48
DDR Museum 40
Denkmal für die ermordeten Juden Europas 24, 34
Department stores 78
Design Center 76
Designer boutiques 78–79
Deutsche Oper 112
Deutscher Dom 26
– Bundestag see Reichstag
Deutsches Historisches Museum 28
– Technikmuseum 84
– Theater 113
Dietrich, Marlene 51
Domäne Dahlem 66, 90
Dutch Embassy 42
East Side Gallery 54
English Theatre 113
Ephraim-Palais 41, 42
Europa-Center 69
Fernsehturm 38–39, 42, 45, 66
Filmpark Babelsberg 95
Fischerinsel 42
Florian 83
Forum Fridericianum 25
Französischer Dom 26
French Embassy 34
Friedrich the Great Monument 27
Friedrichshain 83
Friedrichstadtpalast 112
Friedrichstrasse 25–26, 34

Galeries Lafayette 34, 78
Gedenkort Wiesse Kreuze 55
Gedenkstätte Berliner Mauer 55
Gedenkstätte Deutscher Widerstand 59
Gemäldegalerie 58
Gendarmenmarkt 26, 34
Gethsemanekirche 82
Grunewald 91
Hackesche Höfe 32, 78
Hamburger Bahnhof 63
Haus der Kulturen der Welt 60, 64
Haus der Wannseekonferenz 91
Helmut Newton Stiftung 70
Hi-Flyer 49–50
Hotel Adlon 24, 34
Humboldt University 27, 34
IBA-Hochhaus 52
Inneministerium 64
Invalidenfriedhof 54
Jüdischer Friedhof 81–82, 86
Jüdisches Gemeindehaus 71, 76
– Museum 47, 84
KaDeWe 67, 69, 78
Kaiser-Wilhelm-Gedächtnis-Kirche 45, 68
Kammergericht 47
Kant-Dreieck 76
Karl-Liebknecht-Haus 86
Käthe-Kollwitz-Museum 71

Kempinski Hotel 71, 76
Kempinski Plaza 76
Kino Babylon 86
Klosterkirche 42
Knoblauchhaus 41
Kolle 37 86
Kollwitzplatz 81, 86
Komische Oper 112
Kommandantenhaus 28
Komödie und Theater am Kurfürstendamm 113
Konzerthaus Berlin 26, 112
Köpenick 88–89
Kreuzberg 83–85
Kronprinzenbrücke 64
Kulturbrauerei 82, 86
Kulturforum 56–57
Kunstgewerbemuseum 58
Künstlerhaus St Lukas 76
Kupferstickkabinett 58
Kurfürstendamm 70, 76
Lehrter Bahnhof 61
Literaturhaus 76
Madame Tussauds 25
Marie-Elisabeth-Lüders-Haus 63, 64
Marienkirche 39, 45
Markets 79
Märkisches Museum 41, 42
Martin-Gropius-Bau 50, 52
Maxim-Gorki-Theater 113
Mauermuseum – Haus am Checkpoint Charlie 55

Mauerpark 54
Mies van der Rohe 59
Ming Dynastie 42
Mühlendammbrücke 42
Museum Berggruen 74
– Blindenwerkstatt Otto Weidt 32
– für Film und Fernsehen 49
– für Fotografie 70
– für Gegenwart 63
– für Gestaltung 59–60
– für Kommunikation 50
Museumsinsel 29–31
Musikinstrumentenmuseum 57
Neue Synagoge 33
Neue Wache 27–28
Neues Kranzlereck 76
Neues Museum 31, 66
Niederkirchnerstrasse 52
Nikolaikirche 41
Nikolaiviertel 41
Oberbaum bridge 83
Olympiastadion 46, 67, 75
Opera 36–37
Opernpalais 28, 34
Oranienburger Strasse 32
Oranienstrasse 83
Pariser Patz 24–25
Park am Wasserturm 66
Park Kolonnaden 52
Parlament der Bäume 55
Parochialkirche 42
Paul-Löbe-Haus 63, 64
Pergamon Museum 31–32

Pfaueninsel 91–92
Philharmonie 57, 112
Postfuhramt 32
Potsdam 92–95, 96
 Dutch Quarter 92–93
 Kolonie Alexandrowka 93
 Old Town 92
 Schloss Cecilienhof 95
 Schloss Sanssouci 93–95
Potsdamer Platz 46, 48–49, 52
Prenzlauer Berg 80–82, 86
Prinzessinnenpalais 28, 34
Quadriga 24
Raum der Stille 34
Reichstag 47, 60–63, 66
Renaissance-Theater 113
Rosa-Luxemburg-Platz 86
Rotes Rathaus see Berliner Rathaus
Sammlung Scharf-Gerstenberg 74
Savignyplatz 71, 76
Schaubühne 71, 113
Scheunenviertel 32
Schlachtensee 67
Schloss Bellevue 64
Schloss Charlottenburg 66, 73
Schlossbrücke 28–29
Schlossplatz 29
Schwules Museum 85
Senefelderplatz 86

INDEX

Shopping 78
Siegessäule 60
Skate by night 66–67
Sony Center 49
Spandau 89–90
Spree 64
St.-Hedwigs-Kathedrale 26–27
St.-Matthäus-Kirche 59
Staatsoper Unter den Linden 27, 34, 112
Stadtmauer 42
Steiff in Berlin 67
Story of Berlin 71
Swiss Embassy 64
Synagogue 82, 86

Tacheles — Interntionales Kunsthaus 33
Tempodrom 52
Theater am Potsdamer Platz 112
– des Westens 76, 112
Tiergarten 64
Tilla-Durieux-Park 52
Topographie des Terrors 50, 52
Turkish Market 84
Unter den Linden 25, 34
Volksbühne 86,
Viktoria Park 83 113

Volkspark Friedrichshain 83
Wall 54–55
Wall Trail 54
Wannsee 67, 91
Warenhaus Tietz 42
Wasserturm 82, 86
Weinhaus Huth 46, 49
Wilhelmstrasse 34
Willy-Brand-Haus 52
Wittenbergplatz U-Bahn 70
Zeiss-Grossplanetarium 82
Zeughaus 28
Zoologischer Garten 60

General Editor: Barbara Ender-Jones
Editorial assistant: Petronella Greenhalgh
Research and coordination: Alexandra Achermann
Layout: Luc Malherbe, Matias Jolliet
Maps: , JPM Publications, map.solutions GmbH, Berliner Verkehrsbetriebe (BVG)
Photo credits: hemis.fr/Frumm p. 4; /Guiziou pp. 8, 30, 62; /Borgese p. 46 (Jüdisches Museum); /Torrione p. 78; /Guglio p. 105. istockphoto.com/Hulton Archive p. 11; /typo-graphics p. 12; /Schuster p. 18; /muffinmaker p. 23; /Hiob p. 36; /Fitzer p. 37; /naphtalina p. 44 (TV tower); /dystortia p. 45 (Berliner Dom); /caitrionad p. 47 (office buildings); /podgorsek p. 47 (Reichstag); /agphotographer p. 66; /dirkr p. 108; /goldhafen p. 117. Marc Michel pp. 16, 25, 33, 81. Peter Scheu p. 20. Florence Minder pp. 26, 49, 57, 60, 75. Alexandra Achermann pp. 39, 44 (Marienkirche), 46 (Französischer Dom), 51, 54–55, 61, 67, 79, 85, 94, 101 (top and bottom), 103, 104, 107, 114, 120. Bildagentur Huber/Gräfenhain pp. 40, 44–45 (Quartier Daimler); /Lawrence p. 69; /Müller-St p. 106. Frankinho p. 72. fotolia.com/ArTo p. 50; /Neuhauss p. 89. Jon Smith p. 92. Ständige Vertretung p. 98. Stephan Gustavus, Friedrichstadpalast p. 110. Staatsoper Unter den Linden p. 112. Sarah Arlen p. 118.

Copyright © 2009 JPM Publications S.A., 12, avenue William-Fraisse, 1006 Lausanne, Switzerland
information@jpmguides.com – www.jpmguides.com

All rights reserved. No part of this book may be reproduced or transmitted in any form or by any means, electronic or mechanical, including photocopying, recording or by any information storage and retrieval system without permission in writing from the publisher.

Every care has been taken to verify the information in the guide, but neither the publisher nor his client can accept responsibility for any errors that may have occurred. If you spot an inaccuracy or a serious omission, please let us know.

Printed in Switzerland – 12844.00.5007, Weber Benteli/Bienne – **Edition 2009**

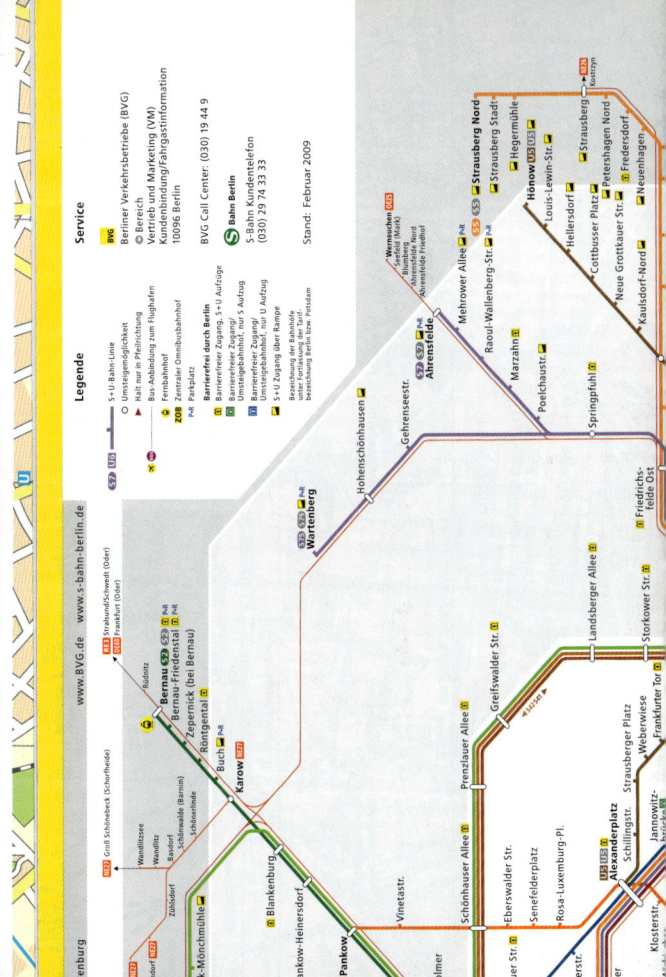